Praying for England

Praying for England

Priestly presence in contemporary culture

Edited by
Samuel Wells and
Sarah Coakley

continuum

Continuum
The Tower Building, 11 York Road, London SE1 7NX
80 Maiden Lane, Suite 704, New York NY 10038

www.continuumbooks.com

First published 2008

British Library Cataloguing-in-Publication Data
A catalogue record for this book is available from the British Library.

ISBN 978-05670-3230-0 (paperback)

Typeset by Kenneth Burnley, Wirral, Cheshire
Printed and bound by MPG Books Ltd, Bodmin, Cornwall

Contents

Introduction: Prayer, Place and the Poor   1
Sarah Coakley

1   Representation   21
Stephen Cherry

2   Glory   41
Peter Wilcox

3   Imagination   65
Samuel Wells

4   Presence   85
Edmund Newey

5   Attention   107
Jessica Martin

6   Honesty   125
Andrew Shanks

7   Debate   147
Grace Davie

Epilogue   171
Rowan Williams

Four Poems   183
David Scott

A Note on the Littlemore Conference   187
Samuel Wells

List of Contributors   191

Index   195

Introduction

Prayer, Place and the Poor

Sarah Coakley

Introduction: Priesthood

This book is written in an attempt to reimagine the place of the Church of England in today's 'secularized' culture. But more particularly it is written to reflect on what priestly ministry can, and should, mean in such a culture. The group of younger priests who met to struggle over, and pray about, such questions started with a grander undertaking: we wanted to think about how the 'imagination of the nation' could ever be recaptured for the gospel – a challenge that had been laid before the Church by Rowan Williams at his consecration as Archbishop. What we discovered, in the course of a very memorable first meeting together (punctuated by regular periods of prayer and worship, and greatly assisted by ecumenical, lay and religious interlocutors), was that there was something else we had to tackle first. We had to do nothing less than reimagine *ourselves* – our own priesthood, and its extension to the 'priesthood of all believers' – before we could effectively reimagine the wider problems of Church and culture. And this is what this book is about.

It might seem otiose, even pathetic, for priests to spend time wondering about what they are and do: is it not obvious what sort of jobs and roles they are meant to be getting on with? And is it not equally, and painfully, obvious that any *social* status they may have enjoyed in earlier generations as a result of these jobs and roles has been largely eroded? The popular media image of the male clergy diverges paradoxically and revealingly: either as the harmless and incompetent figure of fun (the 'ice-cream jacket' type), or as the sinister and seductive schemer (the 'black beetle' type). Either way, the office of priesthood comes under critical, even demeaning, public gaze. (*The Vicar of Dibley* adds a certain canny resourcefulness to the female image, but with no obvious hint of underlying holiness.) Yet as Grace Davie points out, in her sociological contribution to this book, there are actually profound theological gains to be made in a situation of secularization and derision. There are particular undertakings, she argues, that only a *weakened* established church can engage in, and thereby with renewed creativity and insight. There is, for instance, a delicate public brokerage to be achieved between the country's increasingly impassioned and divided religious voices, one that goes well beyond the tired 'lowest common denominator' model of earlier 'liberal' negotiation; and the remaining existence of establishment precisely allows and supports this possibility of reasoned exchange. Andrew Shanks, too, reflects on the opportunities afforded by the *loss* of an assumed ecclesiastical privilege: there is a call, he says, to radical honesty, radical self-examination; uncomfortable truth-telling is one of the key prophetic burdens of ministry.

To find spiritual opportunity in loss or humiliation is one strand that unites these essays, then. But it would be a mistake to hear this theme as priestly self-flagellation or as a settling for hopelessness. Rather, it is just one dimension, but a key one, of the probing of the priestly vocation *as hope* that is attempted here. At its best, such faithfulness in humiliation is Christlike; its quiet patience may do more to convert the scoffer than tactics of denial or *riposte*. But it has to be accompanied by other commitments, equally subtle and often unremarked upon; and it is the task of this book to reflect on them. There is, for instance, in priesthood

– as Jessica Martin so searingly describes in this book – the sheer discipline of 'attention', of staying even with what is unbearable and intractable and not looking away. There is too the *shaman*'s role of accompanying the dead on their last journey, and thus negotiating the fine line, the threshold, between life and death. As Edmund Newey puts it in his chapter in this volume, we might call this unique priestly task a '"recollection forward" – a reaching out from our home in time to an eschatological "home" beyond time'. It both plays with time and puts time in its place.

The priest's role, in these and other daily responsibilities, is always more demandingly *representative* than might seem obvious. In an established church, in particular, the dog-collared figure bears more weight of expectation and longing (or alternatively, of revulsion and loathing) than he or she may consciously know. The priestly office, even in secularized Britain, still comes with such burdens and possibilities. Thus Sam Wells recounts how, in prayerful 'godly play', the priest has the representational power to unlock a congregation's imagination – to release a whole community's sense of the transcendent impinging on them, empowering and enabling them even in an apparently hopeless social setting. Worship can thus become the setting of transformed 'socialist' resistance. Peter Wilcox reflects on the parallel ritual dramas of football and church. Here too the 'football-mad' priest can move across worlds, sharing the sense of 'glory' and transcendence that football at its artful best mediates, but representing at the same time, precisely as a fellow fan, a judgement on football's 'darker' sides. Finally, Stephen Cherry tells the story of the costliness of this priestly form of 'representation' at a time when a body is (literally) torn apart. It is the parish priest's job, even in the most unchurched society, to witness publicly to horror and to refer it liturgically to the place where alone it can find meaning – in the broken body of Christ.

When priests efficaciously enact their priesthood, then, there is this quiet quality of vicariousness or 'representation' in what they do. It is a demanding, and often discomforting, place in which to stand. Whether one is on the 'Catholic' or 'Protestant' wing of Anglicanism (and our group contains all sorts, as well as being challenged and goaded by ecumenical interlocutors) there is an acknowledgement of this 'liminal' sensibility – of its power, and of its danger. But there is also a sense in which this representative function may rightly remain somewhat invisible or untheorized: as has been sagely remarked by the anthropologist of ritual, Catherine Bell, the ritual actor is effective precisely if and when *unconscious* forces are released, and that is why there is a limit to the analysis of the action that can take place. For the Christian priest, that release is one signal of the activity of divine grace; yet the attempt to manipulate it is fatal. One can only gently receive it and deflect it back to its proper goal (and source) in God.

If we begin to think in this way about priestly representation, then it may be possible to see also, by extension – as Grace Davie hints later in this book – why an issue as explosive and unresolved in our culture as homosexuality may in England have to be painfully debated and played out precisely in the context of the *Church*. Derided and laughed at by the secular press, the Church's anguished (and often unedifying) division nonetheless 'represents' a wider cultural *aporia*. As such, the debate cannot be hurried or quickly foreclosed: it is a painful process, unsolvable by false bids for power or fast attempts to capture the moral high ground.

The representational 'invisibility' of priesthood in a secular society thus can, paradoxically, be its true strength. Needless to say, this role often does not *feel* strong. It is a matter of theological virtue (faith, hope, love) rather than perceived victory. Maybe we should think of it as roughly akin to the main drainage system, a metaphor used more than once in our shared discussions together. Like the main drainage system, the Church of England and its priesthood can still be taken for granted in secular Britain. Like the main drainage system, its efficacy is as deep as it is also invisible. Like the main drainage system, it continues to attend to what often cannot be mentioned. And like the main drainage system, when it goes wrong there is a horrible smell that affects everyone.

The outside observer of Anglicanism might be forgiven for thinking that the current worldwide ructions about homosexuality are what constitute such a 'horrible smell'. In the remainder of this Introduction I shall argue otherwise. The danger of a 'horrible smell' comes more insidiously from another quarter, rarely acknowledged. It comes from a potential loss of commitment (under the pressures of fast contemporary life and the frenzy whipped up over the worldwide 'Anglican crisis') to certain classic disciplines of the 'invisible' parish priesthood: the commitment to prayer, to place, and to the poor. These are fundamental, albeit uncelebrated, hallmarks of priesthood everywhere, and not just in the Church of England. But in an established church they arguably have a remaining and special significance for national life on which I now wish to reflect. In the course of the reflection we shall see that – perhaps unexpectedly – the three hallmarks belong intrinsically as a package, and so stand and fall together. But more significantly it is the first one, prayer – the *most* 'invisible' of these three invisible disciplines – that sustains the whole priestly edifice. It is also the discipline most insidiously in danger of erosion.

Prayer

It has taken me nearly 15 years of living in the United States – a country so variously and luxuriously and even worryingly 'religious' – to comprehend the special quality of this low-key English connection of prayerful 'presence', 'place', and ministry to the 'poor'. Had I not lived for all these university years in North America (returning to Oxford, and latterly to my parish assignment in Littlemore, only in the summer months), I would not have thought, either, to braid these three *particular* features of Anglican tradition together as distinctive and precious. I might not have thought them into the same box at all. Nor is it – I trust – an impetus either of young (or old!) 'fogey-ism' that has made me see them differently from the geographical vantage-point of America. It is just that the history of religious 'freedom' and pluralism in the United States has created such an entirely different spiritual sensibility from the 'rooted' one (however underacknowledged or despised) that exists in England. My concern for this English rootedness is, however, emphatically not *nostalgic*: it is as much about the present and the future as it is about the past. For it is about those aspects of Anglican religious life which, if abandoned, would quietly but quickly spell the final destruction of a central core of religious identity reaching back to, and indeed behind, the Reformation. (That is why no Anglican jingoism is either intended, or implied, in what I write; it is precisely here that we are most indebted to our Catholic heritage.) In the United States, with its much-vaunted separation of church and state – constantly rhetorically announced, if not always consistently honoured in practice – there is necessarily no 'established' church, no national parish system, and therefore no historic link back to an originally monastic sense of geographical 'stability'. This makes a difference of subtle, but enormous, proportions. Both the topography of church architecture in a town or city, and the sense of optionality, transience and choice in religious matters, are thus quite differently nuanced from the way they are in England.

In what follows I sketch out some brief remarks about each of my three topics, and then – by means of a parish *vignette* – rebind them together again to indicate how, in the English context, the sum of them is seemingly more than its parts.

Prayer, first. Sometimes I fear that English Anglicanism has given up on holiness. I hope and trust that this is not so, but in my gloomier moments I wonder. I note now that many, even most, advertisements for new Anglican incumbents seek a minister who is gifted in 'leadership', or one who is 'energetic' and 'efficient'. Rarely do they ask for one who is 'prayerful' (would this be regarded as precious or élitist?). But this ecclesiastical trend towards secular models of personal efficacy is odd; for if ever an age yearned for authentic sanctity, it is surely ours. Think of the magnetism of John Paul II, of Mother Teresa, of 'Father Joe'; think of the well-documented current quest for 'spirituality' over institution. And think of the unerring capacity of even the hostile secular press to sniff out the evidences of the ineffable characteristics of personal sanctity. Is it then that there has somehow been a tacit conclusion that Anglican sanctity is *impossible*? Has the business-inspired model of 'leadership' completely supervened over spiritual authority? Is Anglican priesthood set on a false self-abnegation which corrodes the very possibility of its renewal?

Some characteristically bold words of Evelyn Underhill to Archbishop Lang on the eve of the 1930 Lambeth Conference are worthy of repetition, and seem as fresh as ever:

> May it please your Grace: I desire very humbly to suggest with the bishops assembled at Lambeth that the greatest and most necessary work they could do at the present time for the spiritual renewal of the Anglican Church would be to call the clergy as a whole, solemnly and insistently, to a greater interiority and cultivation of the personal life of prayer ... *God is the interesting thing about religion, and people are hungry for God.* But only a priest whose life is soaked in prayer, sacrifice and love can, by his own spirit of adoring worship, help us to apprehend Him.

The apparent clericalism in Underhill's words may strike some as offensive. Surely the clergy cannot bear this responsibility to prayer alone, and does not everyone know by now that the laity is often more 'soaked' in prayer than its harassed and overworked (albeit 'efficient') 'leaders'? Yet surely Underhill is nonetheless right about something basic: without the daily *public* witness of a clergy engaged, manifestly and accountably, alongside their people, in the disciplined long-haul life of prayer, of ongoing personal and often painful transformation, the Church at large runs the danger of losing its fundamental direction and meaning. It has lost the public, and therefore densely symbolic, manifestation of the quest for holiness to which *all* are called. And it should never be underestimated with what longing the laity look to the clergy for an example in this matter. It is perhaps not so significant *how* the priest exercises this charism (and evangelical and 'catholic' wings within Anglicanism will of course have different views and practices); but I am personally concerned, as others are, about the creeping loss of the shared commitment to the daily office as at least a fundamental anchor in what should also spread out into further personal prayer and intercession for the parish. Within Anglicanism a daily Eucharist has of course never been the norm, except in larger Anglo-Catholic parishes. But with the increasing erosion of Morning and Evening Prayer as well, there is no *public* witness to the clergy putting this task first in their hierarchy of 'business'; more insidiously, there is a drifting away from the centrality of the prayer of the Psalms and from the constant – sometimes creatively jolting – input of the weekday lections.

It may be objected that as more and more parishes share a minister, and as more and more parishes rely on non-stipendiary priests who have other day jobs, this *desideratum* has become in practice impossible. This is certainly a challenge (though not, I think, an insuperable one, once the extension of this key responsibility is made to the laity, especially to some of those who are retired). The more insidious and underlying complaint, however, is that it is pointless to pray office in the church if no one else comes *except* the priest. I do wonder about the real impetus of this (regularly expressed) objection: is it that the clergy have stumbled on the true 'impossibility' of prayer, and fallen at the first hurdle? We think of R. S. Thomas, daily and consistently throwing lonely prayers against the cold walls in his 'The Empty Church':

> Why, then, do I kneel still
> striking my prayers on a stone
> heart?
> (R. S. Thomas, *Later Poems: A Selection*,
> London: Macmillan, 1983, p. 108)

Yet a crucial answer is given, even within the terms of Thomas's peculiarly bleak apophaticism, in another of his poems ('Adjustments'):

> Patiently with invisible structures
> [God] builds, and as patiently
> we must pray, surrendering the ordering
> of the ingredients to a wisdom that
> is beyond our own. We must change the mood
> to the passive . . .
> (R. S. Thomas, *Later Poems: A Selection*,
> London: Macmillan, 1983, p. 113)

'We must change the mood to the passive' (Thomas). 'God is the interesting thing about religion, and people are hungry for God' (Underhill). The loss of disciplined clerical prayer in a busy age is fatal: for the priest, for the priests' people, for ecumenical relations, and even for national life. Its absence is – quietly but corrosively – devastating. In contrast, its faithful presence (even if *felt* as 'failure', as the flinging of prayers on a 'stone heart') can be nothing short of electric. The problem is that we clergy are often the last people to realize what has been lost when we abandon it.

Place

But what, second, does this matter of clerical prayer have to do with geographical 'place'? Is it not just talismanic or superstitious to think that prayer in the church building makes a difference?

It is another difference, of 'free market' religiosity in North America, that has drawn my attention newly to this question of Anglican architectural and geographical 'orientation', and its strange relation to the matter of clerical presence and prayer. The fact that Anglican parish churches still provide the central architectural focus in villages, small towns and parts of larger cities is not something to be dismissed lightly. Often at the axis of the meeting of roads, the church building is also at the crossroads – whether consciously or unconsciously to the local inhabitants – of many singular moments of decision, change or transition. That moments of rage and frustration should attach to it as much as moments of celebration or grief itself witnesses to the church building's dense symbolic power, its status as what Jean-Luc Marion would call a 'saturated phenomenon' – one endowed with an 'excess' of meaning. The pelting of the church or vicarage with stones, eggs or other missiles (as happened a few years ago over several weeks in the parish of Littlemore) is, in a strangely back-handed way, also an implicit quest for narrative meaning, a demand that some social ill be attended to. That the vicar at the same time is deemed personally implicated in this dis-ease, along with the church building, is manifestly painful, but not a matter of random chance: the priest's presence, prayer and witness are again being called to account.

Sociologists of religion point to a paradoxical state of affairs in current English responses to religious place. On the one hand, much of what I have earlier called the 'American' feeling of optionality, choice and fluidity in religious 'preference' is fast becoming a feature of English religious life too: many (so-called) 'secularized' people prefer to step into a cathedral occasionally for a good liturgical show rather than make commitments to their own parish church which might be burdensome. To that degree the tradition of immediate *local* religious 'rootedness' is eroded. On the other hand, precisely this draw to historic 'holy places', or to scenes of fatal accidents or special celebration, has seemingly become the more accentuated in our culture, and has re-emphasized the importance of place in a new way. Something of this paradox is memorably evoked in Graham Swift's novel *Last Orders*, in which the entirely secularized friends of a deceased butcher take his ashes on a pre-planned pilgrimage to cast them into the sea, but unaccountably find themselves making an impromptu visit to Canterbury Cathedral on the way, the casket dutifully in hand. They are not quite sure why they are there, but somehow it seems necessary and appropriate. They shuffle around a bit, in a slightly awed and embarrassed way, but then get back into the car and drive on to the coast.

John Inge has written recently of how the importance of place, and especially of 'holy place', is always such because of its association also with *people*: 'Places exert a profound effect as a result of our encounter with them *and* with their inhabitants' (*A Christian Theology of Place*, Ashgate, 2003, p. 130). Any church building shelters many such memories: of past clergy, holy and not-so-holy; of remarkable 'saints' amongst the congregation, perhaps only fully recognized as such in their passing (her laughter

> got under the skin of suffering
> and put it in its place

writes David Scott of one such whom he buried); of joyous and tragic moments of transition in the lives (and deaths) of people whom we have loved. It is as if the building itself holds these memories of people from the past, and acts as a kind of spiritual incubus for the coming 'Church triumphant'. Past, present and hoped-for future blend as memories are re-cast in the context of a consecrated building.

Dietrich Bonhoeffer, writing to his young fiancée Maria von Wedmeyer from prison in the increasingly bleak summer of 1944, struggled to explain how he could now think of the power and importance of his own past, yet in a way that did not bind him to it, or in any way spoil his present love for a woman so much younger than himself. 'We must continually bathe all that is past in a solution of gratitude and penitence', he wrote (gently rebuking Maria for thinking that the past had little obvious efficacy) . . . '[T]hen we shall gain and preserve it . . . That is how, without tormenting ourselves, we can look back on the past and draw on all its strength. God's grace and God's forgiveness preside over all that is past' (*Love Letters from Cell 92*, HarperCollins, 1994, p. 193). A man of Bonhoeffer's spiritual stature could say this of himself, as he began to acknowledge the possibility of his own imminent death. For many of us, it is in special 'holy places' of association that we begin to glimpse the possibility of such a 'bathing' of the past in 'gratitude and penitence'.

'The church is not a building.' That is most certainly true. But buildings in which 'prayer has been valid' are more like people than stone or brick, because of their vibrant association with the folk we and others have loved. They are not so much haunted as 'thin' to another world in which past, present and future converge. And when, as in the parish system in England, each such building holds the memories of a particular geographical community, it is as well to be aware of its remaining symbolic power – even if it now seems neglected, under-used or actively vandalized. To pray in such a building, faithfully day by day, is to continue to participate in the *grateful* 'bathing' in the past in which Bonhoeffer engaged (after all, in even more desperate circumstances than ours), and constitutes in itself an act of hope and love for the future. Such a commitment gets to the heart of 'sustainability' in a community more incisively, perhaps – albeit intangibly and mysteriously – than any political or ecological survey can. And such faithfulness to a 'place' will also be sure to lead to meetings with those members of the community who have been pushed to its edge, and who see in the church building some last-ditch potential for aid.

The poor

It is here, then, that we move to the last – initially perhaps less obvious – point of connection: to the poor. For some, perhaps, it might be wondered afresh who the poor are in contemporary Britain. Apart from knowing that they are 'always with us', who are they exactly? These can only be questions of the privileged. Suffice it to say that the priest who faithfully prays in his or her church building day after day will have no trouble discovering who the local poor are. *They will find the priest.* Romantic views of the poor invariably miss the point – as well as evading the exhausting and repetitive challenges posed by those who constantly arrive seeking help (or dispensing insults) at the sacristy threshold and on the clerical doorstep. The grieving, the distressed, the insane, the homeless, the abused, the drug- and alcohol-crazed, the recently imprisoned, the political refugee or the simply unchurched and desperate together present huge difficulties – and increasing physical dangers – for any incumbent. The problem of safety for women priests working on their own is particularly worrisome and acute.

But the point I wish to make here, once more, is that the contrast between North American religiosity and the English parish system is, in response to such need, again quite striking. The historic American vision of a Church as a pure 'gathered community' – or (in sociological terms) as a 'voluntary association' (Talcott Parsons) – creates an entirely *different* understanding of 'charity' or social alleviation than does that of a national church; and this sectarian backcloth rubs off to a significant degree on American Episcopalianism also. (The case of American Roman Catholicism is complicatedly different, but I cannot here digress to comment on it.) During the university year I am an Associate Priest in the parish of the Good Shepherd in Waban, Massachusetts. When a needy or deranged person arrives on the doorstep of this parish in the leafy outskirts of Boston (an eventuality which, revealingly, does not happen very often at all: such is the covert, but rigid, *apartheid* system of American suburbia), the supplicant expresses no implicit sense of national *right*. It is worth a try to see if the rector or his assistant will oblige with aid, financial or otherwise; but he or she fully expects to be seen off expeditiously in order not to 'spoil' the beauty and order of the liturgy!

The atmosphere and expectations could hardly be more different in my summer parish in Littlemore. The mental hospital up the road, alone, supplies us with a never-ending stream of curious, desperate and hopeful visitants. Disaffected, druggy or merely bored village adolescents are also more than merely passers-by – though they are more inclined to express their feelings about the significance of the site by vandalizing the churchyard than by attending a service. All this is before we get to the many young unmarried mothers in the village, the divorced or separated, the unemployed, the depressed, the grieving, the sick and the frail. The sense of 'right' that such folk have in belonging to the church is palpable; and this is particularly true of the patients from the hospital, even if the police occasionally have to be called to sort out a disturbance during a service. Littlemore

Hospital, to its great credit, has become accustomed to providing nursing aides for those psychotic patients who long to come to church but cannot cope on their own. The liturgy thus often borders on the chaotic, a fact of which I myself am not particularly proud! Yet there is no doubt that this church is for everyone; and that among the most desperate are those who find particular meaning in the daily access to the clergy in office or quiet weekday Eucharist. Some will say: 'I can't face a crowd, but this I can manage.'

And this brings me to the close of my argument.

Prayer, place and the poor: a Littlemore requiem

I have attempted, in this introductory chapter to our shared volume on contemporary English priesthood, to capture something of the *distinctiveness* of what we perhaps still take for granted in the Church of England without ever really celebrating it. (If the drains are working, we hardly need to 'celebrate' them.) Encoded here in the parish structure of English Anglicanism, as I see it, are at least the remnants of the possibility of a true religious socialism, a sense of a 'living nation' responsible for the whole. Roman Catholics, the Orthodox, and the Free Churches may baulk at this idea, thinking that this is perhaps the last, pathetic gasp of a false Anglican fantasy of hegemony. But it has been the burden of this chapter to suggest that Anglicanism's historic privilege to pastor the 'nation', and its simultaneous commitment to prayer, place and the poor, has now of necessity become a shared and *ecumenical* endeavour which nonetheless only an 'establishment' (weakened though it is) has the remaining power to propose and foster. The stakes are high, because the spiritual need is great. 'Praying for England' is indeed a demanding and ongoing task.

One person, now dead, has taught me more about this braiding of prayer, place and the poor than any other, and I end with a reflection in his memory. His story is not one with a good ending (at least, not in this life); indeed, it ends about as badly as it possibly could do. What this man taught me is that a priest can't 'fix' things. She or he can pray and can remain insistently faithful to a place and to a needy person; but the rest is often out of our view. This last consideration in no way invalidates the other ones.

'Steve' (not his real name) was a Littlemore resident with a ferocious and immovable depression. Not without natural charm or talents, his life had nonetheless somehow been derailed at the outset, his sense of selfhood crushed and debilitated by an unhappy and ultimately broken home. By his late forties, Steve had given up on the possibility of a stable job, despite a spell in the Army as a cook and several other periods of temporary employment. He took to hanging out at the morning office at the parish church, and to ringing up the vicar on a daily basis in the afternoon, pathetically asking for help, and wallowing in self-pity. Despite much encouragement, he would never come to the main Sunday services to enjoy the wider fellowship or to receive Communion, nor would he accept any *practical* offers of assistance. The Vicar, Fr Bernhard Schünemann, decided to offload this exhausting charge onto his new summer curate (me), in the hope that some special pastoral attention over a few weeks might shift something.

Taking care to get proper supervision from the chaplain at the mental hospital, I embarked on this task with some diffidence and caution, meeting with Steve for an hour two or three times a week, after morning office. But I need not have worried. Steve had the most natural and perfect sense of proper 'boundaries' of any parishioner I have ever encountered. The practical problem of where we should have our meetings (it being, I thought, improper for us to meet alone in the church) was graciously solved by the Roman Catholic Sisters of *das Werk*, who agreed that I should meet with Steve in Newman's library in the College (just opposite where Steve lived). This illustrious *locale* provided some moments of high farce, as well as of profundity: I well recall the morning when Steve proudly brought in his saxophone and broke the contemplative quiet of the College with his rendition of 'Strangers on the Shore' (not half bad, actually). And something like a minor miracle was already happening, quietly: Steve stopped moaning incessantly about his past and his family, and started to show an extraordinary gift for extempore prayer. At the start of every meeting I would pray for him first, and then turn to him and say 'Now you'. To begin with, it was all gloom and doom, but over the weeks his prayer transmuted into compassionate intercession for others in need in the parish, and for the agony of the world at large. This new form of prayer even spilled over slightly into his inputs to the morning office in church, greatly surprising the other clergy. Early on, it had occurred to me to ask him, in the midst of Steve's usual recitation of past miseries, if he could remember any time he had really been genuinely and completely happy. Steve answered immediately, and without missing a beat. 'Yes,' he said, it was the day that he'd taken up the challenge to do a parachute jump for charity, and in the moment that he was pushed out of the aeroplane and took flight, leaning into the wind and feeling the 'chute bearing him up, he'd known the most glorious ecstasy in all his life. This moment became thereafter the metaphoric touchstone in our discussions. When I finally persuaded Steve to come to the main Sunday Mass one week, he arrived late, crashing through the west door just as I was turning around at the altar singing the *Sursum Corda*, my hands raised. The next time we met, Steve was emphatic: 'I saw you there; you were parachuting . . .'

When the time came for me to return to Boston at the end of that summer, Fr Bernhard and I had carefully prepared Steve for my departure. All along I had feared that this special attention that had been devised for him might lead to a dependence, or that he would interpret my exit as another betrayal. But again we had underestimated him. There was a little service of anointing and blessing, attended also by the Sisters, and Steve was cheerful and upbeat. He had even promised me he would consent to seeing a doctor again about the depression: better drugs than Prozac were, after all, now available. But over the next year, while I was back in Boston, things apparently went downhill dramatically. Steve's bedridden mother was finally taken into a home, and this was a point of no return: his life unravelled for the first time into actual alcoholism and begging on the street. One of the last times I saw him alive was at the conference at Littlemore that has spawned this book; he appeared outside the College dishevelled and crying, asking Rowan for a blessing.

In the cold Lent of the following year, the police found Steve dead in his squalid little cottage. Although he had long stopped attending office, the parish church had never given up on him, and Fr Bernhard had only a few days before checked on him and taken him food. Even the Bishop, Richard Harries, had tried to help, miraculously supplying a replacement saxophone for Steve's own, which had been stolen in a street scuffle. Only after the autopsy was it revealed that he had died of a drug overdose, presumably acquired from squatters whom he had invited in to share his quarters. Sister Mary at the College, knowing I would be devastated, wrote gently to remind me that this was not the end of Steve's story, and that they were praying for his soul at the College. After a bit of a tussle and considerable diplomatic manoeuvring with the divided family, Steve's body was released from autopsy and his funeral conducted in the parish church on the morning of that Maundy Thursday.

When I think, now, about the connection of 'prayer', 'place' and the 'poor', I inevitably think of Steve. Yet I think not of what I tried to give him (which was little, temporary and – as it turned out – woefully inadequate), but what he showed me. In his 'parachuting' mode Steve grasped the centrality of the *orans* posture, the absolute indispensability of prayer: at least once in his life he had experienced the ecstatic 'free fall' into the wind of the Spirit. He also knew that the parish church of Littlemore was *his*, his 'place', even though his wretchedness was so great that he had come to refuse the sacraments and finally to push away all those who repeatedly tried to help. Finally, he showed me that it is preposterously false to think that we clergy can 'fix' the poor: it is more truly they who 'fix' us, by reminding us of our endless need for grace and our empty-handedness without it. In showing me this, Steve showed me Christ.

As I write this, Steve's ashes have, I believe, still not found a resting place. My hope and prayer is that he will finally be brought back to lie in Littlemore graveyard. It is his 'place'. It is perfectly true that his story is still unfinished. Sister Mary was right about that.

*   *   *

Bibliographical Note

'Secularization' is initially used in this Introduction in inverted commas, since its meaning and use is now so debated: Charles Taylor's recent *A Secular Age* (Harvard University Press, 2007) comments incisively on its ambiguity, noting that a dramatic loss of church membership does not necessarily imply a lack of restless questing for spiritual meaning. Catherine Bell's *Ritual Theory, Ritual Practice* (Oxford University Press, 1992) provides a wonderful analysis of the complex power of ritual, its capacity to hold together, and transform, 'impossible' tensions. John Inge's *A Christian Theology of Place* (Ashgate, 2003), and John Rodwell's 2007 Reckitt Lecture ('Remembering the Land', forthcoming) illuminate beautifully the religious issues of 'place' and 'sustainability', respectively. Finally, Michael Hollings' *Living Priesthood*

(Mayhew-McCrimmon, 1977), ch. 2: 'Priest, Person of Prayer', says better than anything I could ever express what is crucial about the personal prayer of the priest.

Chapter 1

Representation

Stephen Cherry

This chapter offers a stark and searing account of what priesthood can mean in a secularized and sometimes violent culture. It reveals that the parish priest still acts as a representative figure through whom a community is able to stay with a time of unspeakable horror. It is a story of dismemberment, and of how, through a ministry of presence, patience and liturgical leadership, a priest can enable a shocked community to re-member not only a person but also its sense of goodness and wellbeing. This is not an account of how a priest 'fixed it' or turned darkness into light, but of how faith was embodied and communicated through patient listening, ritual action and the ability to stay still.

Calling

One afternoon in November 2002 I received a telephone call from a local radio station. The hasty reporter asked if I was prepared to give an interview about the body parts that were being found. I was very puzzled: 'What body parts?'

'An arm of a teenage girl was found in the canal and no one knows who it belongs to,' came the answer.

'In Loughborough canal?' I was astonished.

'Yes, they are looking for the rest of the body but no one has been reported missing. Can you talk about it?'

'I feel I need some time to absorb this,' I replied. 'Is that all the information you have?'

'That's all we know. We need someone to give a reaction to this. Can you do it?'

There was a long pause.

'Okay. Phone me back in ten minutes.'

In the silence after I put the phone down, I prayed. A thousand scenarios presented themselves to me. My mind was quickly in chaos and I was intensely anxious about what would unfold and what could possibly be said about it – and how people would react.

This is how the darkest and most demanding ministerial experience of my life began. And it was as well that I took the time to pause and think because it was not long before my world was a whirl of phone calls, visits, interviews and encounters with deeply distressed individuals. Trauma had come to Loughborough, and as a parish priest I was involved in a way that was both prominent and ambiguous.

I did the interview. It must have been obvious that I was shocked and yet I sought to give a sense that I was somehow coping with the shock. I was also tentatively aware that we may not yet have heard the worst in this case. As we heard the news, we were all bracing ourselves for what was to come. Arms don't just get detached from bodies. Something had happened and real people were involved, people who have families and friends. Then I started to think of the people I knew who lived near the canal. I made some phone calls to see how they felt. In the early evening I visited the pub on the bank of the canal just where the arm had been found. When I arrived, it was more or less empty but Sky TV were about to interview the landlord. I pulled up my coat to hide my clerical collar from the film crew and spoke with the few people who were there. We shared our inability to respond. But the numbness was somehow comforting.

Overnight, more body parts were found and I received an early phone call from the radio. The victim was not a girl but a boy. Another interview followed. No content, just 'reaction'. At one level it was an exercise in saying nothing. I felt that my role was to articulate the pain, the horror and the ambiguity. And to do this I had to inhabit a situation that was deeply unpleasant and uncomfortable. But I felt it to be a priestly calling to immerse myself in this. And as I did so, some words ran through my mind – words which I had read in the extraordinary memoir of the philosopher Gillian Rose, *Love's Work*. The words are those of Staretz Silouan: 'Keep your mind in hell and despair not.' They are the opposite of common sense but for me they seem, on reflection, to have been prophetic for the way in which I would engage with the horror that at this stage I was only beginning to glimpse. Or, to put it in more ordinary terms, after that first interview there was to be no running away. And this was because I was engaged here not on my own behalf, not as a private individual, not as 'me', Stephen Cherry, but as some kind of public representative figure. I had become a mouthpiece for a stunned community but also a kind of mirror to that community. As people heard me saying some of the things that they were feeling, there was a resonance that was comforting, which began to give a sense of community. Like the shared numbness in the pub.

It was only a matter of hours before there was a call to appear before television cameras. A BBC crew was coming to film not from the canal but from where the investigation was currently taking place. Realizing that time was briefly on my side I said I wanted to think about it. While I was thinking, I phoned the diocesan communications officer for her advice. She suggested that I phone the police. I did so straight away and found myself talking to a Chief Inspector whom I had last met when he was reading a lesson at our Community Carol Service. I explained what I felt my emerging role was and how I did not want to do or say anything that would make life more difficult than it already was. He did not have much by way of advice but clearly appreciated being asked and said he would discuss this with the officer responsible for the investigation. This was the beginning of a relationship with the police that weaved through this whole story and which, from my point of view, was always positive.

The media were gathered at the epicentre of the search for remaining body parts and other evidence. This happened to be immediately outside the primary school which my children used to attend. It was a sad and chilling spectacle as officers in white boiler suits approached a plastic bag with caution and reverence. Then they explored inside it. We learnt that it contained blood-stained clothes likely to fit a 14-year-old boy. We all breathed a sigh of relief that it was nothing 'worse'. Then I was interviewed. It was a very short interview – two questions, two answers. One of the answers was broadcast several times. In it, I said how uncomfortable everyone was feeling and that, while people were not saying so in so many words, you could see it in their faces and their gestures. It was true. Everyone was visibly shaken. Including me. And I guess that I was aware that the viewer would be able to detect the discomfort in my own face and that, as with the radio interviews, they would hear a voice that was unsettled. When I saw the clip I realized that mine was definitely not a knowledgeable or 'in control' voice. Nor was it a 'caring' voice. It was a troubled voice, and I was a troubled person, a troubled parson.

Later that day I gave a long telephone interview to the local weekly newspaper. This was a great challenge. It is so hard to convey sensitivity in print. Towards the end of the telephone interview I was asked whether 'the church' would be doing anything to respond to this. Having done little else for two days I was slightly taken aback. But what the question meant was, 'Will the parish church building be at some point a place of spiritual hospitality for people who have been disturbed by this event?' I was reluctant to commit to this. As yet we did not know who the victim was. If any church event was planned *before* the identity was revealed and yet took place *afterwards*, there could be all sorts of complications. Not everyone wants to be associated with the Church, and at times of grief and death one has less right than ever to make assumptions about people.

But in a few reflective moments after the interview I changed my mind. The key factor was the connection between the Church – represented by the parish church building – and the shocked and disoriented population of the town. I phoned the reporter back and said, 'Yes, the parish church will be open all day on Friday. People can come and be quiet for a while or light a candle or whatever.' But there was a pragmatic matter as well. I knew that if I said this now it would be on the front page of the local paper the following morning. This would be then the beginnings of an answer to the obvious question – what can be done in response to the fact that a boy has been found in pieces around our town? The answer: people can go to church.

The following day, Thursday, I was back in the school. The headteacher took me into her office and told me that the dead boy was a former pupil who would now have been in Year 9, had he not been excluded just over a year ago. Extraordinarily, I had been in the school on the day he was excluded. I recalled the long conversation with her about it, in which I had begun to glimpse the depths of the personal agony that comes along with making such decisions. I even remembered the boy's name. He was Adam. Adam Morrell.

At lunchtime Adam's name and a photograph were released to the world. A police officer called me to ask about what was planned for the church. He was with Adam's mum and she wanted me to know that she was pleased that we were having the church open and planned to come along at some point during the day.

Of course people came along to church on the Friday. Some came with flowers, one or two with other little tokens, and all with heavy hearts and confused minds. There were many tears. I put out a few sheets of paper on which people could write notes of condolence. This was very popular. Volunteers from the congregation appeared and we were able to serve coffee and tea at the back of church all day. Most people lit a candle on arrival, and then offered a silent prayer. Many then just hung around for a while. Some came to the back of the church for tea or coffee as they relaxed a bit.

A major worry was how to cope with the media interest in the day. When it came to it, however, everyone was keen to honour my plea and not do anything that might make life even more stressful for grieving children. To help them do their job, I let them film and photograph me lighting candles at a time when no one else was about. I felt pretty uncomfortable about this, but the images of flowers and lighted candles that were projected from the church gave a welcome relief to the stark ones of the canal being dredged or police in white boiler suits searching in bins for evidence. And once again it was not about me: it was about the rector of the parish church lighting a candle which was at once for Adam and for the town.

Community

Every funeral is a work of art. There is a form, there are expectations and there is creativity. Funerals speak to the heart, touch the imagination, engage the emotions and abide in the memory. But more than this, funerals are always 'community art'. They are never the work of one creative genius working alone and delivering a product to a waiting audience. They are prepared by a process which involves not only the 'funeral visit' but all sorts of other conversations and encounters.

In this way Adam's funeral, six months after his death, was like any other. It was carefully planned, but it did not consist of the words on the page of the service sheet. Rather, it was an event that was made up of all the various elements that came together on the day. It was like a carnival, if one accepts that a carnival has its darker side; that among the celebrations there is an acknowledgement of some of the dread, the menace and the dark side of life.

At the Parochial Church Council meeting during the previous week we had been able to spend time on the question of hosting the service. We agreed that our recently established practice of providing a 'welcome team' at weddings and funerals would stand us in good stead. However, we felt that we would need to provide a much bigger team than usual. In the end there was a team of about 20 people on duty. Quite a number were stationed outside the church. Curiously, much of the PCC discussion had been about the badges that members of any welcome team would wear. This was something we had not yet settled but which was forced into focus by this funeral. The decision was that the badges should be large and bear the name of the church, a logo and the word 'welcomer' or 'steward'. This was very satisfactory and established that wearers were in role as representatives of the church as they directed people, reassured them and generally created an atmosphere that said, 'Yes, we are ready for this event. Together we will get through it.' The church choir turned out too – and robed. There was no request for choral music but they were there to honour the occasion. The day was a very poignant one for the town, the community and therefore for the church. The unspoken feeling was that the whole church needed to be 'at home' to welcome and support the mourners. We were making the statement that this loss, this tragedy, this grief is shared. It was not the occasion merely to provide a venue or to calculate 'who needs to be there' but 'how we can best express our solidarity, our fellowship with those who feel most deeply and personally what we are all feeling generally'.

A key aspect of our spiritual hospitality was in terms of consciously inviting God to be part of the proceedings. And so it was that a small group gathered at 9 a.m. for a Communion service in the chancel. It was very moving in its simplicity. The Eucharist is the most profound way of facing the realities of evil and death – both of which were very much on our minds as we anticipated the arrival in church of a coffin bearing the remains of a dismembered boy. Never has the moment of the fraction, the breaking of the bread, been more central in a service or more real. 'We *break* this bread.' And the crisp, round disc is cracked in half. Yes, bodies do break; they are broken. And when they are, it seems as if the world is falling apart. And yet this moment is at the heart of our redemption. It is the turning point where death and evil are not victorious but vanquished. The bread and wine were shared, generously given and gratefully received. This eucharistic moment brought the light of divine transformation to the gloom of despair and emboldened us to allow the tragedy of Adam and the victory of Christ to sink yet more deeply into our hearts. As we fed on it in expectant silence, we prayed that it would sustain us through the day.

A few minutes before 12 o'clock the deeply apprehensive silence around the church was broken by the unmistakeable sound of horses' hooves on tarmac, and then, under the trees, the hearse appeared. Television cameras and newspaper photographers jostled for position in the small area set aside for them. It was time for deep breaths and deliberate calm. The undertakers did their usual business with trestles and flowers, and as the clock struck midday we were at the church door ready to go. I nodded to the trumpeter, one of Adam's teachers, and he and his saxophonist friend started up with 'When the Saints'. They led us into the packed church where the atmosphere was an extraordinary blend of death and defiance, tragedy and triumph.

To help people focus in the prayers, candles had been placed in all the pews. The plan was that we would light these candles in a certain way. Adam's parents' candles would be lit from the church's paschal candle. Then, the light would be shared from these to all the other candles until the whole church was filled with pinpricks of light. But this is not how it worked out. Certainly we lit those two parental candles with great and deliberate care. But when I looked up, I saw that many people had simply got the cigarette lighter out of their pockets and lit their own candle and passed the light on from there. It was at that moment that I felt that the funeral was 'working'. The people present were taking ownership of it. They might not have been singing the hymns like Methodists but, given the opportunity to participate, or even to take things into their own hands, this is exactly what they did. Anyway the candles were lit, and for the prayers they were held up high, a defiant, triumphant, hopeful gesture.

As the service came to an end I walked slowly and deliberately to stand next to the coffin which stood on trestles at the crossing in the middle of the church. I gently placed my hand on it. 'Let us commend Adam to the mercy of God, our maker and redeemer.' The rubric suggests a silence at this point, but I was concerned that with such a lot of people present on such a charged occasion this might not be possible. But as I stood there, central but quite motionless and silent, so the church became absolutely still. All the shuffling, fidgeting, sniffling and sobbing stopped. It was utterly, peacefully silent. There was a palpable sense of common humanity as we were aware, as never before, that we were gathered around the deliberately, violently and horribly broken body of a child. But it was a transcendent moment too, mirroring the fraction in the earlier Eucharist. By facing the horror of Adam's story together and in church we were beginning to overcome it. We were commending Adam to God and in so doing were drawing closer to God ourselves. I have often reflected on the spiritual power of that moment and wondered about the paradox of priestly or presiding presence. Certainly I was at the focal point of a large and emotional gathering. But I was not the subject of anyone's attention – my own included. That was on Adam and on God.

The service was quickly over and we left the building. Outside, the cameras were busy again. The coffin was put back in the hearse, and the cortège made its way out of the churchyard and into the streets. It was to follow a police car along the police-approved route to the cemetery. Traffic wardens appeared at every junction to wave us forward without delay. One thing that I had not thought about was how all the unaccompanied children would get to the cemetery. The answer was simple: they walked behind the hearse. There were loads of them carrying flowers, glad to be out in the open air, 'stretching their legs' as their parents might say. I wished that I was also stretching my legs, and part of me wanted to jump out and join them. That was where the action was now. But I decided that I was in the right place. They did not need my company or support at this point. They were following Adam and being together.

Witness

The trial took place a year after Adam's death. But if a funeral is a piece of community art, a trial is a costume drama. The courtroom is a theatre of justice and the principal characters wear costumes and perform. I sat in the public gallery along with Adam's parents, a few friends, some family members of the defendants and such police as were needed to observe the proceedings and keep the peace. Immediately in front of us were a few journalists. Opposite us was the jury. The judge introduced the trial and gave the jury members some idea of what to expect. We eyed them carefully, wondering if they were trustworthy, whether they were up to the task, whether they would do justice. As we stared at them – and we were all doing it – we saw them turning paler and paler. To the right was the dock. It was empty now but the next day they would be there: behind counsel and behind a glass screen. For one it would be his birthday and all of them were already a year older than they were when Adam died: two 19-year-old boys and an 18-year-old girl.

Before the jury was elected there was a suggestion that some of them might be given dispensation not to sit if they were afraid that the gruesome nature of the case and the evidence might upset them. The judge, his black cap placed carefully on the table in front of him, dismissed this contemptuously. That black cap is a strange thing, carried in along with his white gloves. I asked about this and was told that the death penalty was still on the statute books, but only for treason. But the black cap got me thinking. Suppose the death penalty were an option. How would that influence the way we looked at those people behind the glass? How would it influence the way evidence was presented and heard? How would it impact on Adam's parents' feelings? How would it impact on this drama if the ultimate sanction were not 'life' but 'death'? The dynamic would be quite different. The stakes would be much higher, the 'justice' have more power to satisfy the wrath that had been generated. One of my predecessors as Vicar of Holy Trinity, Loughborough, the Revd Bernard Wright, was a prison chaplain, and as part of his duties had accompanied prisoners to the scaffold. He recorded all their names, 21 of them, in his Prayer Book and remembered each of them on the anniversary of their death. One day while taking an early morning Communion service he stopped as if stunned. It was the anniversary of one of 'his men' – and he had forgotten. He was mortified and took some time to recover. For all the harshness of his role he was a sensitive man. His career as a prison chaplain came to an end when he had to accompany a woman to the scaffold. He could not stomach it any more. He had seen enough.

I attended as much of the trial as possible. Having had such a prominent role the previous November and then at the funeral, it was odd and unnerving to have no official role at all. And in some ways this made attending the trial the most demanding priestly role that I played. But maybe it was also the most significant. As I sat in the court or mingled in the café in my black clerical shirt and a white collar, I was an object of curiosity. 'What's the vicar doing here?'

The opening speech from the prosecuting counsel set the scene. It was lengthy and detailed and carefully revealed layers of evidence relevant to the charges of murder and perverting the course of justice. We heard for the first time of the pathologist's report. In terms of 'bruises, scratches and abrasions' there were 76 on the one arm that had been recovered, 60 on one leg and 78 on the other. There were 52 on his torso, which also had a 'wet burn mark'. There were 14 areas of injury on his head. There was a rib fracture but no skull fracture. There was no evidence of a sexual attack but there was evidence of strangulation. There had been considerable bleeding from the jaw and cheek and within the heart. There was bruising to the neck and haemorrhaging of the eyes. Some of the marks on the body were 'gripping marks' and it seemed that he had been picked up and dropped repeatedly. Other marks suggested that he had been punched, others suggested slaps, and others kicks. There was considerable swelling of the brain. Such was the extent of internal bleeding within his head that his scalp had lifted away from his skull.

It was at this point that Adam's mum bolted for the door.

Then we heard about the skin loss to the torso caused by the burns. This was not a normal scald mark but worse. Not only had boiling water been poured onto him but it had been previously mixed with sugar. The syrup which resulted retained its heat and stuck to the skin. All these injuries had been inflicted over an extended period of time. Most had been sustained some hours before his death. It was a 'prolonged and vicious attack' lasting a day or more.

During the trial, the details of what happened to Adam were repeated more than *ad nauseam*. But what made people especially sick was the thought of him incarcerated for a period which no one could precisely specify, much of it in a 'pulverized state' while the others, who had started on the beating while under the influence of drink and cannabis, paused to go to Loughborough Fair, get more drugs and shop for cleaning materials. That and the fact that it was impossible to identify a motive.

When the defendants were in the witness box, more details were added to the story and more images conjured to haunt the mind. Distinctions were drawn between 'football kicks' and 'stamps'. We heard of the already badly beaten Adam being carried to the toilet to be sick and we had the image of him being kicked from a chair to the floor only to be picked from the floor, replaced on the chair and kicked off again. The defendants described Adam as 'unrecognizable' and 'looking like an alien'. We were told that he 'cried his eyes out'.

On the day of the verdict, I rushed to the court to join the family queueing to get in to the court as soon as it was open. We waited. We went in. We waited some more. The court assembled. The judge appeared. The jury foreman got up to speak. We did not know whether to look at the foreman or the defendants. I knew that some were eyeballing the defendants with hostility, daring them to be found not guilty. The foreman announced that they found Matthew Welsh guilty of murder. And from behind me an utterly visceral, heartfelt and heartrending shout of 'Yes!' went up from Adam's dad.

After that, the court quickly cleared. I loitered around for a while and spoke with police and counsel about the whole business. I had had many passing words with them over the previous weeks but it was difficult to talk about things in any detail while the trial was going on. There was a sense of relief that it was over, that there was a murder verdict. One officer wanted to talk about how God could allow such suffering, about whether there was an ultimate justice, about whether the guilty would in the end be absolutely sent down. I did the best I could, but it was not a time for rationalizing. Emotions were running high. What came across most surprisingly, however, was a consistent theme of gratitude that I had been there. I had received some intimations of this over the previous weeks. There was a feeling that it was appropriate, right and helpful that a priest – a stranger wearing a black shirt and clerical collar – was there in the public gallery just listening to it, witnessing it. I was aware that some felt that I had been a comfort to the family – but this was not primarily about being a pastor or a counsellor. It was not about helping but sharing, acknowledging that this had happened, hearing the story. And just as part of the purpose of the funeral was to affirm Adam's dignity and individuality as a child of God, so my presence at the courtroom was about affirming and acknowledging the depth of his suffering. In this I was God's representative, God's witness. This was a deeply uncomfortable role, and I struggled in it. The whole experience touched me, overwhelmed me, wounded me. As I walked away at the end of each day I felt as if, like Jacob, I was limping. That may be claiming too much, but I am a different person for having sat through all that; more of a priest, perhaps.

Imagination

Adam was murdered just four months after Jessica Chapman and Holly Wells in Soham, and the trial of his captors and murderer took place at the same time as that of Ian Huntley and Maxine Carr. However, whereas the Soham story was headline news, Adam's story failed to catch the imagination of the nation. This was hardly 'the nation's' fault. Rather, it was a product of the amount of media exposure. Adam's imprisonment, torture and murder was, as the local paper put it, 'Loughborough's worst crime' but even as the Soham trial was at the top of the national news, the trial of Adam's assailants was kept off the teatime bulletins as the details were too disturbing. In the end a strange combination of gender (male), age (adolescent), background (there were no happy pictures of Adam to hand to release), grim reality (extended beating, the sugar solution torture and dismemberment) and lack of a motive contrived to hide Adam from the attention of the nation. This is hardly surprising – we hear of very few of the children who are lost or murdered each year. But this truth reinforces the significance of the attention that the Church might be able to give in such situations. As we heard, felt and acknowledged Adam's truth, so we were affirming his dignity and humanity – and ours.

It was my intuition of this need for acknowledgement that encouraged me to respond to the call to commit my time and energy to the ministry that unfolded after Adam's arm was found in the canal. It has also informed my decision to attempt to narrate it here. It is of course *my* version, *my* perspective. It is also an edited story and it takes care not to describe the aspects of it that were essentially private and intimate conversations. These should be remembered, because representational ministry does not take place in a pastoral vacuum any more than in isolation from an ordinary, living Church. On the contrary, personal conversations with Adam's parents, meetings with police officers, visits to various schools, random encounters with strangers in the street, adults and children, those who knew Adam personally and those who only read the papers, added up to a very sizable assignment over the year or more of this 'episode'. Because it was so public, the ministry impinged on many relationships. The representational nature of the work also impacted on my reputation in the town, my image. This exposure elicited surprising and humbling support. Numerous phone messages, kind words from strangers, and even some cards from individual members of other churches all offered gratitude and promised prayers. It became clear that others were identifying with this ministry. This, I felt, was more than encouraging: it was authenticating. For it was not 'my' ministry at all but Christ's, mediated by an accessible, recognizable and authorized representative.

The representative role is as old as the hills. Austin Farrar was alluding to it when he spoke in an ordination sermon of priests as 'walking sacraments'. The priest is a sign, a symbol; in a contemporary sense, an icon. The parish priest is to be *seen*. But the representative role is not a contradiction of the many other ministerial roles and responsibilities that are a necessary and integral part of the life of the Church as it serves the mission of God. On the contrary, the lived representational role has a dynamic that creates ministerial opportunity. The priestly vocation is to open up space in which others can be healed, transformed and called (not necessarily in that order).

I certainly had a major role, both in public and private, on the day of the funeral; for instance, it was quite clear that the work of Christ's ministry was not carried by an individual but by a community. The presence of the 'welcome team' at the funeral had an enormous impact on the atmosphere both inside the church and, more significantly, outside, where several were stationed. The kindly face in the churchyard or at the church door was as much the face of Christ to the grieving as was any robed figure. The person sitting near the church toilets was just as much a 'minister' as the person leading the prayers. This sense of shared ministry in the face of such raw anguish had a significant impact on the congregation and on its self-understanding, not least in its ongoing hospitality to those most deeply touched by this tragedy and by extension to the most vulnerable members of society.

And yet it is the person in the role of the parish priest, the representative minister, who catches the imagination. But this is neither a matter of regret nor of celebration. It is just the way the imagination works. It has often occurred to me that the parish priest features in the public mind in a similar way to the parish church. Both are seen positively in their own right but both are also lenses through which more important realities can be glimpsed, for instance hospitality and prayer; that is, both the candles and gravitas at the front of church and tea and lightness at the back. But the priest and the building are also windows onto God's grace and glory – the one a walking sacrament, the other a stone one, but both capacious, generous and solid. And both are often more understood by the world than the Church.

Harrowing

One of the ironies of representing the Church in such challenging circumstances is that precisely as the ministry impinges on you most deeply as a person, so you can become, by ministering so publicly, less of a subjective and more of an objective presence, less of a familiar person and more of an archetype. This is an especially costly reality for those who feel called to a pastoral ministry based on inter-personal sensitivity, empathy and compassion. But it is also difficult for those who are not sufficiently self-aware or secure in their faith to realize that they have an image or 'reputation' which is way beyond their own control. But the minister needs to remember that the repeated appearance of one particular vicar's face in the paper is not a welcome sight in every household. To be a representative minister is to be publicly and privately criticized, resented or feared by friend or foe – as well as by fellow ministers, lay or ordained. It is equally true that one can be unreasonably and unhelpfully admired, respected and appreciated. But either way, the representative minister, the authorized public Christian, the priest, carries a continued exposure to the fantasies and fears of others, most of whom are unaware of the extent to which their feelings are perceived.

Some clergy feel especially confident wearing their clerical shirts and collars – whether it is in accompanying police in body-armour on a walk around a housing estate or stepping into the middle of a knife fight in a town centre, as a colleague did recently. But others feel that the role makes them vulnerable. Idle comments from passers-by: 'More tea vicar?', 'Let us pray' and so on can be unnerving. But niggling as such things can be, they pale into insignificance alongside the account of a colleague who, on visiting a working men's club as a curate, was asked whether she was the stripper. The anecdote is excruciating. But the question can point to a deeper truth, that the parish priest is not only an 'office holder in role' but also of a 'vulnerable human being like you'.

Throughout the experience of ministry around Adam's death I was aware of considerable anxiety, uncertainty and discomfort. It was so hard to know what to do, what not to do, how to priori-tize. The chaos unleashed by an event of this kind, motiveless torture and murder, is profoundly disorienting, and as one enters into its reality so one is drawn into a very dark place, a very deep struggle. To say that I was outside my 'comfort zone' is true but banal. To call it a place of 'agony' is getting more like it, for there was both anguish and struggle. But to call it 'harrowing' is, I believe, both emotionally and theologically correct. Theologi-cally, because it is a journey with Christ to what can only be thought of as hell on earth. Emotionally, because one enters not wearing spiritual body-armour but as a human being like all the others involved. Inevitably, such a harrowing ministry had a significant impact on our domestic life. This was epitomized for me when, during the funeral, I looked up in the first hymn to see my daughter halfway down the packed church. I had not expected her to be there; she did not know Adam. 'But Dad,' she said afterwards, 'Adam has been such a big part of our life this last six months; I felt I had to be there.' I was taken aback. But it was true. Representational ministry in such a situation – which can happen anywhere, any time – is a role which is not easily contained within the bounded orderliness that is often prescribed for ministerial life.

My wife was a member of the 'welcome team' at the funeral. As the church emptied of congregation after the service and a few people were tidying up, she was overwhelmed by a flood of emotions and burst into tears. She wept. But these were not merely personal tears; they were the tears of our household, 'rectory tears'. They were a release from the emotional and spiritual hospitality that had been extended to the tragedy and grief of Adam's murder. And in that moment of release, as a few took turns to comfort her, there was a new appreciation of the weight of the burden that the months of this ministry had involved. It was a cathartic moment and an occasion of transformation. Many people grew in faith and ministry that day. A few hours after the funeral, I received a phone call from a member of the church who was checking that I was 'okay'. That had never happened before. But such hidden ministry is also representative of the love of Christ and the purpose of the Church. It is such ministry that affirms both our common humanity and the vulnerability that comes with it.

To say that the day of Adam's funeral was a dreadful encounter with the pain of the world is of course true. But what I have narrated here is not a day's work or a specific occasion; it is an episode which lasted more than 12 months and which was alive in the mind years later. Taken as a whole, it seemed to me that to engage in this ministry was truly to share in Christ's harrowing of hell on earth. It was not so much a long Good Friday as a slow Holy Saturday.

This returns us to a final point which, like so much here,

derives from what seems to be an accident or coincidence. In this case, Adam's name. In the Hebrew, 'Adam' is not only the first man but the primordial, definitive human being who is 'of the earth' (Genesis 2.7). Paul refers to him as 'the man of dust' (1 Corinthians 15.47). The theological connections that flood out when one thinks of Adam as *both* this particular tragic adolescent *and* as the representative human being are never ending. They certainly inform the way in which I now read the Bible, and hear the word 'Adam' in both Old and New Testaments. I have come to think that while it is our baptismal project to become more Christlike, we can only do this while being open to the truth that there is an essential Adam-likeness in Christ. The second Adam was, in terms of vulnerability, as Adam-like as the first, as Adam-like as all human beings.

It is Adam-likeness which underlies and authenticates representational ministry, true priesthood, which, even while it is mediated by a particular fallen human being, a 'me', remains a manifestation of the grace of God. In the Adam-like Christ, God is in a compassionate, earthy, healing solidarity with humanity at its most vulnerable and tragic. This is what representative ministry is saying to the world. And its method? To seek out the company of 'Adam' wherever Adam may be and to enter into that relationship with both Adam and Christ which is at once harrowing and yet also the basis of resurrection, which feels like hell but is at the gate of heaven, which might look like a lonely individual taking an important role but is in fact the action of the Church in partnership with its crucified, risen and ascended Lord.

Chapter 2

Glory

Peter Wilcox

At the centre of the Church's life is worship. But people worship in ways other than through recognized religious leaders and acknowledged liturgical buildings. Perhaps no other activity has such a hold on the imagination of all social classes in England as football. If the glory of God is a human being fully alive, then there is much to celebrate in the aura that surrounds football. Yet the Church is unclear whether to regard football as a healthy form of leisure and athletic activity, as a parallel place of belonging amid social atomization, or more sinisterly as a rival religion with its own gods, its own liturgies and its own consequent idolatry. This chapter portrays the cultural and imaginative power of football and reflects on whether the Church (and the priest) is lost amidst it, or on the way to rediscovering a more popular sense of glory.

Football is a phenomenon. In the United States, admittedly, 'soccer' is a Cinderella sport, raggedly junior to baseball, basketball and American Football. But even in the US, the 'Beautiful Game' has a large and growing following; and almost everywhere else in the world it is the First Sport – the one most people watch, both live and on television; and the one most people play, if 'knockabouts' in parks and gardens are included in the count alongside more organized expressions of the game. It remains the only truly worldwide sport, played as 'our game' in Africa (north, south, central and west) and America (North and more especially South), Asia (especially in the south east) and Australia, Europe and the Middle East. The qualifying competition for the 2010 World Cup will involve a staggering 204 countries, and television coverage of the 2006 competition was broadcast to no fewer than 214 – whereas the United Nations has only 193 member states.

In Britain, football is unrivalled in its popularity. On every conceivable scale of measurement it comes out on top: it attracts more participants, more supporters, more television coverage and pages of newsprint, and many times more money than any other sport, and more even than any other art or leisure activity (including gardening and home improvement, and with the possible exception of shopping – if this can truly be regarded as a leisure activity). It certainly has a bigger following than politics and religion. It is sometimes said that more people attend church at the weekend in Britain than football matches – but the statistics simply don't bear this out. It's true that only about a million people a weekend pay to watch English professional football, whereas almost as many attend worship each weekend in the Church of England alone. But paying spectators are only a fraction of the total number of those who watch live soccer. Fans of the amateur game must also be counted: parents watching children (some of them forsaking established patterns of church attendance on Sunday mornings to do so), friends watching pub-teams – even passers-by pausing to catch a few minutes of the action while taking a stroll in their local park.

There is surprisingly little theological reflection on this phenomenon. It is an area of growing sociological analysis and reflection – such that, at Leicester University for example, a centre has been established within the Department of Sociology devoted entirely to football research. But as with other intensely experiential phenomena which captivate the imagination of Britain, at least among the under-30s (shopping, reality TV, celebrity, makeovers, clubbing, taboo-less sex), there is little theological engagement with football.

It is easily forgotten that organized football in Britain had its origins in the Church. Many professional clubs trace their origins back to teams run by church youth clubs or men's fellowship groups: examples from among current Premier League sides include Aston Villa, Everton, Liverpool, Manchester City and Tottenham Hotspur. About 100 years ago, Lord Arthur Kinnaird (Lord High Commissioner to the General Assembly of the Church of Scotland, Chairman of the Football Association and player in a record nine FA cup finals) is alleged to have said, 'I believe that all right-minded people have good reason to thank God for the great progress of this popular national game' (cited by Peter Lupson in *Thank God for Football,* SPCK, 2006, p. xv). One wonders what he would have made of its progress over the following century.

Football as religion

If football was ever 'just a game', it ceased to be so long ago. As early as the 1930s, J. B. Priestley observed that 'to think of football as merely 22 hirelings kicking a ball is to say that a violin is merely wood and cat-gut, *Hamlet* so much ink and paper: it is conflict and art'. In the early years of the twenty-first century, in the throes of a revolution brought about by first satellite and now digital television, football is no longer even 'just' conflict and art: it is big business, and it increasingly adopts the language and trappings of a religion.

What constitutes a religion? If a person's 'god' is that which gives meaning to their life, upon which their sense of identity is grounded, which determines their behaviour and around which their life revolves, then a 'religion' is a corporate, institutional expression of such a thing. In these terms, football – or more specifically, football-supporting – is for many a religious activity. Theologians are inclined to point out that etymologically, 'religion' derives from a Latin root meaning 'to bind together': if this is so, it strengthens the case for regarding football as religious activity, since for many fans it is their club allegiance that provides them with their primary community. Their lives are dominated by this sport – or rather, by their fanatical devotion to one particular team.

Equally significant, however, is the fact that football is now deliberately marketed as a religion. In the last ten years, emboldened by the success of televised matches on Sundays, promoters of football and commentators on it have increasingly employed traditionally religious language. Spectating is presented as a form of worship – implying, presumably, that worship is popularly perceived in terms of spectating. The ground is the temple, the stands are the pews, the boardroom is the Holy of Holies, celebrity footballers are gods. ('Come and worship at Anfield this Sunday' is a typical example of the way advertising has developed since the inauguration of the Premier League.) The worship is devout: the chants are sung with arms outstretched to heaven, eyes closed. Hands are clasped together in petition. Of course, many factors have contributed to the overwhelming change in the character of Sunday in Britain over the last 25 years – but the dramatic increase in Sunday football (professional and amateur) is not to be overlooked among them. It has to some extent competed 'head to head' with church for attendance and, as many parish clergy will testify, has 'won'.

Almost 50 years ago, Bill Shankly (legendary manager of Liverpool Football Club) famously remarked, 'Some people think football is a matter of life and death. I don't like that attitude. I can assure them it is much more serious than that.' One man interviewed for a Channel 4 documentary recently remarked that for him football is 'more than a religion, it's a way of life'. In saying so he was incidentally betraying the fact that religion is regarded by many today as a hobby, an 'add-on' which need not interfere fundamentally with a person's lifestyle. For him, football is more basic, central and life-defining. A fan on a Bristol City website writes, 'I am not a religious man, quite the opposite. However . . . It is a spiritual, magnetic feeling being . . . at a game with thousands of other City fans.'

So what is it about football that commands such allegiance and captures the imagination for so many? There are perhaps four things above all: football achieves a quasi-religious status in British society, because of its capacity to provide art, drama, a moral framework and (crucially) belonging.

The art of football
On Tuesday evening, 10 April 2007, Manchester United offered a glimpse of the glory of God.

The quality of their football in the second leg of their Champions League quarter-final match against the Italian side Roma was simply breathtaking. Trailing 2–1 after the first leg in Rome, United won 7–1 at home, to win the tie 8–3 on aggregate. To score seven goals in any professional game is unusual. To score seven in the Champions League, and against Italian opposition, is unheard of. Italian football is strong: its national team are World Champions (characteristically winning a tight, low-scoring final in 2006 against France on penalties). This is the Italian way: polished defence is its hallmark. Roma went into the match boasting the most parsimonious defence in the competition. Yet in a scintillating period of seven minutes early in the match, Manchester United scored three times, playing some of the most memorable football ever televised. The first goal, after 12 minutes, was a thing of simple beauty: a perfectly weighted pass by Ronaldo was collected by Carrick, running at full tilt, and clipped nonchalantly past a startled and stationary keeper. The second goal, five minutes later, was better still: it was the culmination of a move which swept from one end of the pitch to the other. It involved six Manchester United players. Five of them, including Smith, the goal scorer, contributed just a single touch of the ball. 'One-touch football' requires the kind of giftedness and technical ability we might associate with ballet or gymnastics: to see it played at pace at a key moment of an important match, while the game was still in the balance, was a rare delight. To those who watched the match as it was unfolding, it was simultaneously incredible and inevitable that the third goal, a mere two minutes later, should surpass the other two. Again, the move began deep in United's own half. Again, the goal scorer (Rooney, this time) took just a single touch. On this occasion, however, it was the sheer speed of the move which took the breath away: the ball was transferred from one penalty area to the other, along the ground, by six players combining as though choreographed, in just 13 seconds. The star turn was Ronaldo, who ran 50 yards with the ball in the blink of an eye, twisting this way and that to avoid being tackled. To control a ball while running flat out, to be aware of the move-ment of team-mates and opponents, to make decisions in split seconds about where to pass or place the ball, and to be able to execute the decisions perfectly, is exceptionally difficult. The special talent of the world's greatest players is to do this consis-tently and to make it look simple. This is their art, their medium with which to glorify their Creator. Members of the current Brazil team (most of whom are practising Pentecostals, and one of whom, Kaka, takes to the field with an 'I belong to Jesus' T-shirt under his strip) are explicit about this: they mean to 'shine for God' on the pitch.

Football fans watching professional football wait for moments like these: moments of acrobatic, balletic skill; moments when a player exhibits such speed and power, ball control and balance that spectators experience a moment of shared ecstasy. Such moments are not confined only to professional leagues: in parks, even back gardens, gifted players deploy their gifts in breathtaking ways, demonstrating skills worthy of the Creator. Nor are such moments confined to football or even to ball sports. Fans of cricket, rugby and tennis, even of athletics, show-jumping and arguably boxing, have equivalent experiences. Sometimes, in football, it is a feat of individual genius which inspires the fan: mesmerizing dribbling skills, a deft back-heel, an acrobatic shot, a sweetly timed tackle or interception. But what makes most fans purr with the greatest satisfaction is the intricacy of slick teamwork: individuals working together, acting in concert, as if responding to a common impulse, somehow synchronized, creating a shared work of art.

This art is occasionally delicate. Some of football's finest players have been blessed with an extraordinary finesse. (George Best, perhaps the most obvious example of such a player, intriguingly entitled his autobiography just that: *Blessed*.) But speed and power and acute spatial awareness are integral to the art of football. The anthropologist Desmond Morris has argued convincingly that these qualities reveal the tribal origins of the game. Football is, he suggests, a celebration of the arts of hunting and of battle. The prosperity of women's professional football in Britain, and the increasing and successful attempts by clubs to market themselves to families are not to be ignored; but it is still hard to escape the fact that the glimpses of God's glory offered on the football pitch are savoured most by men. This 'Beautiful Game' has been particularly valued in communities historically dominated by harsh (male) heavy industries – in Glasgow, Liverpool, Newcastle, the Black Country and London's east end – or in nations of great poverty, such as Brazil. The caricature of the male football 'fan' is the hooligan: destructive, violent and abusive. For most fans who are men, however, football is an arena in which they are able to express their sensitivity to and their appreciation of beauty. Football is an art-form peculiarly accessible on Planet Bloke.

The drama of football

Since the publication of the Taylor Report (following the Hillsborough tragedy in 1989) and the introduction of all-seater stadia, there has been a massive rebuilding programme of football grounds nationwide. Not least in the way they inspire awe in those who enter them, they are the heirs of the medieval cathedral. The names given to these stadia (which used always to be called after their locations: 'White Hart Lane' or 'St James' Park', 'Elland Road' or 'Goodison Park') are an indicator of the state of the contemporary game. Some reflect the game's increasing commercialization and are named after sponsors: Arsenal's new home is the Emirates' Stadium; Coventry play at the Ricoh Arena; Wigan play at the JJB Stadium. Other names reflect the self-confidence of the contemporary football community: Pride Park in Derby; the Stadium of Light in Sunderland; Liberty Stadium at Swansea. The stadium of Manchester United at Old Trafford is nicknamed the 'Theatre of Dreams'.

One of the extraordinary features of sport is the degree to which outcomes of matches so often feel scripted. Occasionally (especially in recent years, as one of the unfortunate side-effects of the globalization of sport through satellite television) a match is literally 'fixed', usually by an international betting syndicate. But mostly, football is innocently dramatic. Matches which are clearly subject to nobody's control (not even the referee's) unfold in ways that leave spectators enthralled at an apparent scripted-ness. Plot lines are familiar. Among the most common and most cherished (and these clichés are standard in match reports) are: 'David and Goliath' (in which a weaker team defeats a stronger one, especially in cup football, in an act of 'giant killing'); 'the coming of the Messiah' (in which a hero signs for a new club, or returns from injury, makes an immediate impact on the team and leads it to success); 'Judas returns' (in which a hated betrayer, player or manager, comes back to torment a former club, consigning them to humiliating defeat); and 'the Resurrection' (in which a team snatches improbable victory from the jaws of defeat). When Liverpool beat AC Milan in the Champions League final of 2005, to win on penalties after being 3–0 down at half time, newspaper match reports asked 'Who wrote the script?' It's a common question in the mind of the football fan.

Like every kind of effective drama, football draws in its spectators and moves them. In reality, it is always the case with drama that the relationship is not only this way round: performers have a capacity to move audiences, but audiences also have the capacity to move performers, to bring the best out of them or to inhibit them. In football, certainly, the players move the fans; but the fans in turn move the players. One reason why sport makes especially good theatre (apart from the fact that the performance is sheer improvisation within limited rules), is that its fans are partisan. There are two opposing sets of supporters, each with the capacity to contribute not just to the fortunes of a club, but even to the outcome of a match.

For many in our society, football moves people more effectively than anything else. As David Conn puts it in his book *The Beautiful Game: Searching for the Soul of Football* (Yellow Jersey Press, 2004, p. 9), 'Football people are used to it, but it's worth remembering: this is unique in modern life, such an outpouring of noise and passion, so openly and publicly expressed.' The point is worth elaborating. A team's changing fortunes, from moment to moment in a match and from game to game in a season, allow fans to express a range of emotions that for many are only ever expressed in this way. It is a sobering experience for a parish priest in a working-class community to see the same men who sit so impassively in the rearmost pews in church at baptisms and funerals, then singing, embracing or weeping on the terraces of the local football ground. They may not easily 'get in touch with their emotions' at home, at work or in church; but they can do it at the match. In these circumstances it would be no surprise if, when football fans weep tears of joy or sorrow, an immediate victory or defeat is acting as a catalyst to release emotions relating to all life's victories or defeats. Moreover, the fans express emotion in unison: what is striking about the football experience in our society is the way that crowds of 20,000, 40,000, even 60,000 people pour out their emotions together. It is only occasionally at a football match that one is aware of individual voices.

It was a matter of some concern to football authorities, following the publication of the Taylor Report, that the radical changes it recommended might lead to a loss of 'ritual' among football supporters – associated above all with 'the terraces' on which there was standing room only – and a consequent decline in the popularity of the sport. Writing in 1981, Desmond Morris warned, 'Perhaps if the soccer match becomes "fun for all the family" it will lose the very quality which has enabled it to spread around the world and attract larger, more devoted audiences than any other human pastime . . . To turn this symbolic event into Disneyland fun may be to destroy its essential dignity.' But 'perhaps', he continued, 'the reformers who wish to provide modern comforts and efficient organization for the sport will be able to do so without destroying the ceremonial drama of the game' (*The Soccer Tribe*, Jonathan Cape, 1981, p. 317).

Elsewhere in his book, Morris refers to the 'television set' as 'that great social isolator'. In practice, however, the stadium revolution has quite unpredictably gone hand in hand with a television-broadcasting revolution that has resulted not in the dilution and decline of ceremonial ritual for fans, but to its highly effective exportation beyond the stadium. Where one might have expected smaller crowds, with increased viewing of football matches in the privacy of the home, such viewing has instead fuelled a dramatic increase in match attendance, and a furious building programme to increase stadium capacities around the country. Average attendances at Premier League football matches rose year on year between 1994 and 2003 from 24,294 per game to 35,462 (an increase of almost 50 per cent; though they have levelled off since then), and the pattern was repeated (if by smaller percentages) in lower divisions. In addition, the broadcasting revolution has generated an entirely new phenomenon: 'football nights' at the pub. Especially on international and Champions League match days, particularly during European and World Cup tournaments, it has become possible to experience something of the solidarity of a stadium crowd in any wine bar or pub. The crowd (of 20, 40 or even 60), clad in team colours (a sea, often, of replica shirts), may even at times of high excitement in the match break into song just as if it were inside the ground. This success in exporting ritual from the stadium onto the High Street while simultaneously increasing stadium attendances is a challenging one for the Church (coinciding as it has done almost exactly with the relative unfruitfulness of the Church of England's 'Decade of Evangelism' of the 1990s).

The morality of football

There will be more to be said in due course about the ugly side of the 'Beautiful Game' off the field; but the conventions which shape the behaviour of players on the pitch, and the interpretation of their behaviour by fans, are worth considering.

Footballers and their fans can sometimes appear lawless. The point is often made, for example, that footballers compare unfavourably with rugby players (and indeed cricketers) in terms of the way they respond to a bad decision by the referee (or umpire). Rugby players do not contest refereeing decisions. If they do, their team (not the individual) is immediately penalized.

Footballers shouldn't do so either. The rules prohibit 'dissent' and the referee has sanctions he can impose on a dissenting player. Yet it is increasingly common to see a referee besieged by irate team-mates, or subjected to a tirade of abuse by an individual. The fans are as bad as the players: the referee is frequently vilified by supporters during the match, and occasionally has to be escorted off the field of play by police at the end of a contentious game, to protect him from the hatred and violence of losing fans. In 2005, one referee found it necessary to retire from the game after receiving death threats from fans, outraged at decisions he had made in a Champions League game between Chelsea and Barcelona.

Similarly, fans can be extraordinarily cruel in the abuse they hurl at players, usually representing the opposing side, but in extreme circumstances even on their own team. No form of insult is taboo: the harshest imprecatory psalm can sound like a blessing, compared with some of the curses called down on a foot-baller's wife and children by an enraged fan.

The behaviour of footballers also compares unfavourably with that of rugby players in terms of their response to a physical challenge by an opponent. But here, there is a distinction to be made between the players and their fans. Rugby is plainly a more physical game than football: contact is unarguably more brutal. Yet a rugby player is almost never to be found exaggerating injury (quite the opposite) or seeking to con the referee by feigning a foul. Two of the least attractive facets of football today are the tendencies of players both to writhe around on the grass as if in agony after a relatively innocuous tackle (either to waste time or to win the referee's sympathy), only to be running about without any trace of injury within minutes; and to fall to the ground as if shot from behind (usually either to win a penalty or to trick the referee into cautioning or sending off an opponent) when there has demonstrably been no contact. What has been interesting about these recent trends has been the reaction of fans, who are united in their condemnation of 'whiners' on the one hand and 'divers' on the other. Certain players have developed a reputation for cheating, which they cannot easily shed. At least in Britain, Diego Maradona will never be considered the equal of Pelé (the pair are by common consent the two greatest footballers ever), because of the notorious goal he scored with his hand for Argentina against England in the 1986 World Cup Finals. (In his own culture, this incident is regarded not as 'cheating', but as sly cunning and as a blow for liberty and justice struck against the oppressors of the Malvinas.)

Some interesting moral issues are worked out on the field of play when a player is 'on the floor injured'. It has become the convention for either side to knock the ball out of play to enable the injured party to receive treatment. If the player's own team-mates choose not to do so, because they have an advantageous position on the field, that is regarded as acceptable. But if the opposition do it, they are considered to be unfairly exploiting their numerical advantage, and fans of the team which is reduced to ten will whistle and hiss in disapproval. It is also the convention that, if a team does deliberately concede possession in order to enable an injured player to receive treatment, the ball will be returned to them when play recommences. The fans of that team will similarly whistle and boo if this courtesy is not observed. On one occasion, an Arsenal player scored a match-winning goal against Sheffield United when the Sheffield players were passively waiting for the ball to be returned to them. Such was the public outrage that the Arsenal manager was compelled to offer his opponents a re-match. Lately, a further twist in this moral maze has arisen: players are now sometimes deemed to be feigning injury and the need for treatment, in an attempt to force their opponents to sacrifice an advantageous attacking position by putting the ball out of play. Then both sets of fans express their disapproval: one set because they regard the 'injured' player as a cheat, the other because they regard their opponents as churlish, for refusing to create a stoppage in play.

On the other hand, it is possible for a player, once condemned, to find redemption. In recent years, both David Beckham and Christiano Ronaldo have shown this. Both returned to a new season of football in this country after a notorious episode in a World Cup Finals. In 1998, Beckham was blamed for the elimination of the England team at the quarter-final stage, when he got himself needlessly sent off at a critical point in a match against Argentina only to see his team-mates lose a close match on penalties. In 2006, Ronaldo was blamed for the elimination of the England team at the same stage, when he was deemed to have engineered the sending off of an England star, Wayne Rooney, whose team-mates went on, again, to lose a close match on penalties. Both Beckham and Ronaldo returned to Britain to face horrendous hostility from fans. Both were routinely boo-ed at their every touch of the ball in early season games, and both were subject to obscene chanting; Beckham was even burnt in effigy. But both achieved redemption, and ended the season applauded and respected by all. (Beckham's rehabilitation was complete when he scored the only goal – a penalty – as England beat Argentina 1–0 in the 2002 competition: who wrote *that* script?) Their route to redemption was identical: humility and hard work. Both 'knuckled down' to play hard for their team-mates, and refused to allow themselves to be provoked by insult. No doubt both were helped by being extravagantly gifted.

Humility and hard work are lauded as traditionally 'English' values. English fans associate 'diving' and 'whining' with continental (or 'Latin') football and cultivate the myth of the strong, uncomplaining English centre-back or centre-forward, who plays through pain and picks himself up without fuss when he is knocked to the floor. David Winner's study *Those Feet: A Sensual History of English Football* (Bloomsbury, 2005) suggests that these values ('manly mid-Victorian bravery') have been part of English football's essence from the start.

'Football' in England (i.e., the Football Association, the Football League, the Professional Footballers' Association, and the League Managers' Association, together with football commentators and writers) has asserted itself effectively since the 1980s to eradicate racism from the sport. Racist chanting from fans is not tolerated, and black players are valued as much as white ones. The England team has taken the field more than once with a majority of black members. It remains to be seen if and when 'football' will assert itself similarly to address homophobia within the game. At present there is not one single homosexual 'out' in English football. A recent spat involving a football manager's criticism of a female official also suggests that the game has some way to go in removing sexism from the sport.

Football and belonging

The fourth and final respect in which football in England has acquired a quasi-religious character is in terms of the quality of belonging that it effects.

The Department of Sociology at Leicester University undertook a survey of football fans a few years ago, asking them about themselves and the clubs they support. One of the most significant findings was the extent to which fans support a club because it is local. In some communities (mostly in the north, but also including Southampton) over 75 per cent of season ticket holders gave 'locality' and local pride as the explanation for their support of their chosen club. This is not a new phenomenon. Morris put it like this 20 years ago:

> The regular coming together of large congregations on Sunday mornings was more than a matter of communal prayer. It was also a statement of identity. The crowded church service was a

social as well as a theological event. Now, with its passing . . . the urban dweller is increasingly starved of large community gatherings at which he or she can see and be seen as part of a local population. The soccer match has somehow survived these changes and takes on a more significant role as a means of displaying a local allegiance.

This is presumably one reason why 'local derbies' can be so bitterly fought: two clubs are competing for the privilege of representing the same local community. If church was 'a social as well as a theological event', there is also a sense in which a football match is, for the spectators, a theological event as well as a social one.

The extent to which a certain club acts as a vehicle for local and regional ambition varies, but in certain cases it is clear that the football club symbolizes (and acts as a vehicle for the assertion of) the identity of its community. Newcastle United self-consciously projects itself as the flag-bearer of 'the Geordie nation'. There was a celebrated illustration of this in 1998. When it was first erected in the February of that year, Anthony Gormley's sculpture the 'Angel of the North' was vilified by local residents, most of whom could list 100 ways in which the investment in public art might have been better used. But within a few months, Newcastle reached the final of the FA Cup. On the eve of the match, an enterprising fan draped the Angel in a vast black-and-white shirt. From that moment, the sculpture became a truly local landmark: it was baptized and accepted as a Geordie. It now belongs. Over time, the process would doubtless have taken place anyway. But there was something iconic about the image of the statue as a member of the Toon Army which instantly transformed local perceptions of it. Further afield, the president of Barcelona FC is almost *de facto* the president of Catalonia. Similarly, national football teams both reflect and impact upon the cultures they represent, as David Winner's excellent study *Brilliant Orange: The Neurotic Genius of Dutch Football* (Bloomsbury, 2000) and Alex Bellos' *Futebol: A Brazilian Way of Life* (Bloomsbury, 2002) amply demonstrate.

In this first respect, the belonging which fans find in relation to their team or club is something formal and sustained. Fans identify themselves with a club and maintain this allegiance over time: it becomes part of who they are, not only on match days, not only during the football season, but at all times and in all places. In the words of one fan: 'It's my heritage and my roots; City are part of me and my life.' When Sir Bobby Robson finally achieved his lifelong ambition to manage Newcastle United, he told the press (with a reference to the team's playing colours), 'If you cut me, I bleed black and white.' It's a belonging expressed in the wearing of replica kits not just to games, but about town or on holiday abroad. It's a belonging expressed in routinely prioritizing the purchase of a season ticket ahead even of rent or groceries. This formal sense of identity and community which fans find in relation to their team is a form of 'belonging not believing'. Fans often find it hard to account rationally for the intensity of their allegiance: it just is. Significantly, fans who do not support local teams but who choose instead to support the highly successful ones are disparaged by others as 'glory hunters'.

Moreover, in a commitment-shy society, club supporters swim against the tide: they know the cost of discipleship: they give sacrificially, witness to their faith and are persecuted for it by rivals. Fans 'follow' teams as if on pilgrimage. They may even ask to have their ashes scattered on the sacred turf. In these respects, even this formal belonging has a quasi-religious quality.

But the belonging is also expressed in more spontaneous and fleeting ways, on match days and in extreme moments of exhilaration or despair. In such moments, fans testify to a spiritual transcendence in their experience and to a mystical oneness with their companions. In his recent television documentary,

Hallowed Be Thy Game (broadcast on Channel 4 on Sunday, 30 January 2005), Mark Dowd related his own experience, as a fan of Manchester United, at the 1999 Champions League final. The English club was losing 1–0 to Bayern Munich after the full 90 minutes. The German team had dominated the game, and for long periods United struggled to make any impact. But as the game moved to its conclusion, there was an urgency to United's attacking which kept hope alive. The urgency (as well as the subsequent outpouring of emotion) was fuelled by the team's particular history in the competition: they had been favourites to lift the trophy in 1958, when almost the entire team of 'Busby Babes' died in the Munich air disaster; ten years later, the same manager had led the first English team (including legends like Bobby Charlton and George Best) to win the competition. That success meant that the current manager, Alex Ferguson, despite winning multiple domestic trophies, would never stand shoulder to shoulder with Busby, or his team with that one, without a Champions League victory. In the first of three minutes of injury time at the end of the game, United equalized. Then in the third and final minute, they scored a winner. At that moment, Dowd turned, delirious with joy, to his neighbour – a stranger – and embraced him. That moment of ecstatic 'connectedness', of complete mutual recognition and understanding, amounted (he suggests) to a foretaste, a sacrament, of the kingdom of God. In less extreme circumstances, every football fan experiences that connectedness on most match days. It is an experience which offers (in Graham Tomlin's words) 'an intimation of eternity' – a glimpse of God's glory.

Football as idolatry

There is, however, a dark side to this belonging. When individuals identify themselves so strongly and completely with an institution, there is a dehumanizing aspect to the experience and a loss of perspective.

A striking moment in Mark Dowd's documentary came when, approaching fans gathering for a Premier League match in 2003, he presented them with a pencil, and a blank piece of paper bearing an empty circle. He asked fans, if the circle represented the whole of their lives, to shade in the part represented by football. Time and again, they shaded in the whole circle. Often Dowd probed further: 'What about job or family, or other interests? Do they not account for some part of the whole?', only to be told 'No: my life is football.' Perhaps surprisingly, this obsessive fanaticism occurred in female fans as well as male.

Under these circumstances, perhaps societies get the 'role models' they deserve. In a culture in which footballers and other entertainers are paid, each week, two and three times what teachers and nurses are paid in a year, it is not astonishing if their value goes to their heads. It is predicted that the *average* annual pay of a Premier League footballer in the 2007–2008 season will be £1.1 million. Is it surprising if players of the 'Beautiful Game' have an increasingly ugly image off the field? Paid too much too young and treated like gods by fans, professionals frequently find the experience corrupting. In the past few years, several have been charged with rape or violent affray. Their sexual behaviour frequently causes scandal. If not alcoholism and drug addiction, certainly binge drinking and drug use is endemic among them.

Fans too are prone to a loss of perspective. They can be sectarian, frequently exhorting one another to demonstrate their 'love' for their own team by expressing their 'hatred' of a rival. In Newcastle, especially if the team is losing, fans find solace in the chant, 'Stand up if you hate Sunderland.' In Glasgow, it is no longer clear whether the two great football clubs, Rangers and Celtic, express the city's religious divide, or whether churchgoing indicates allegiance to one team or the other. Where once you supported Rangers (or Celtic) because you were a Protestant (or a Catholic), now you are a Protestant (or a Catholic) because you support Rangers (or Celtic).

In recent years, there has been a spate of incidents in England in which players have been hurt during a match by objects thrown from the terraces. Hooliganism is peculiarly associated with this sport. The sociological explanations for why there are no cricket, rugby or athletics hooligans are complex. It used to be argued, by Morris for example, that the issue was straightforwardly one of class: football hooligans are disaffected members of the working classes, expressing frustration at the lack of economic opportunities open to them. But if that was the case in the 1970s, it ceased to be by the 1980s and 1990s, when it transpired that many of those arrested for acts of hooliganism associated with football matches, at home and abroad, were in fact middle aged and middle class. Perhaps the explanation is rather that the hooliganism associated with football reflects its prominence in society. Just as football is the only truly global sport, so the hooliganism associated with it in this country is also found worldwide. It is a more serious problem at present in Turkey, Italy and Holland than it is in England, and there is a history of crowd trouble in South America too. In this country, there is no sport with so many players, clubs or spectators, and as such football perhaps reflects and embodies the culture of our society more than other sports, and not least the violence of our culture.

Conclusions: the Church and football

Soccer-mad parish priests are used to being asked, by disheartened or wistful members of their congregations, 'Why can't church be more like football?' The question may be naïve. It may be silly even. But it ought not to be dismissed too quickly.

Ultimately, it's true, football is entertainment. For all that, it offers scope for art, drama and belonging; its fundamental purpose – for players and for spectators alike – is to entertain. The Church rightly sets its face against being reduced, especially in its worship, to mere entertainment. In discipleship, it champions the involvement of every member and calls on spectators to become participants. There is a universal accessibility to participation in church which is glorious and which football cannot offer.

Yet, at least in the affluent West, the Church is having to learn two hard lessons. The first is that, in a more and more frenetic society, more and more target led and deadline driven, where the pace and stress of life are increasing, 'mere entertainment' is at a premium. Involvement and participation in 'Church' in the broadest sense may be essential to authentic Christian discipleship: but responsibility for the organization of congregational life is not. For 30 years or more, the Church in the West has been promoting 'every-member ministry'. Too often, this has meant little more than an increasing reliance on lay people to organize and deliver Sunday worship (as opposed to the resourcing of the whole people of God in Sunday worship for ministry dispersed in the world, Monday to Saturday). The outcome has been exhaustion. Perhaps one reason why cathedral congregations in Britain have been enjoying a period of remarkable growth during the last decade is precisely that they offer lay people the opportunity to participate in worship without responsibility for organizing or delivering it. True, this is not the same thing as 'entertainment'. But one wonders if those who lead local congregations have fully come to terms with the degree to which the needs of their members have changed in this respect, over the period in which football has so flourished.

The second hard lesson the Church in the affluent West is having to learn at present has to do with the professionalization of leisure activities. As recently as 50 years ago, not least in football, 'Amateurism' had only positive connotations and 'professionalism' mostly derogatory ones. Now the situation is exactly reversed. Nor is it just the playing of football that has been professionalized: the promoting of it has been too. And such has been the flow of money into the game in the last 30 years that everything is now of the highest quality. From replica kit to stadium toilet facilities, from television coverage to club websites, fans have come to demand the latest and best. Church may not be entertainment; but in common with other voluntary organizations, it is finding it necessary to move from 'amateurism' to 'professionalism'; and it is finding the transition difficult.

There is a debate in football circles about what has been lost in this transition. There is some nostalgia for the days before football was 'all about money', for the days when a player might be loyal to a single club for an entire career, when English clubs fielded teams comprising almost exclusively English players. It is widely accepted that the increased wealth in English football has led to its 'gentrification': Roy Keane famously derided the passionless support of Manchester United's 'prawn-sandwich eating' fans. In the 1970s, the staple stadium diet of the football fan was the meat pie. Keane's remark simultaneously highlights both the new middle-class dominance of the football crowd and the abiding passion of the working-class fan. Nothing engages the male residents of England's council estates like football: not work or family, not education or exercise, and certainly not church.

An individual priest with a passion for football is likely to find that the sport impacts on the priesthood in a number of ways. In the first place, the experience of attending football matches (or even watching them in pubs and bars) inevitably drives home the extent of the gulf that exists between the Church of England on the one hand and the council estates of Britain on the other. Generalizations are dangerous, of course; but the football-loving priest will almost certainly struggle to hold together two apparently polarized communities: the predominantly working-class, male and 'under 40s' football crowd on the one hand, and the predominantly middle-class, female and 'over 50s' church congregation on the other.

However, for many such priests (usually themselves from middle-class backgrounds, often still Oxbridge educated), football is also part of the way in which they are able to 'belong' in an Urban Priority Area (UPA) environment. This is not just a matter of finding a shared interest with those among whom they are called to minister (in the way that a devotee of a particular TV programme like *The X Factor* or *Big Brother* might find it the basis for conversation – although football can certainly be that). It is rather that (just as a clubber might find in clubbing, or a fan of the Arctic Monkeys might find in going to gigs) football becomes the gateway into a community. Immersion in 'football culture' through attendance at matches equips a priest to be at home, to belong, in company which would otherwise remain foreign, and which spills out from the dedicated environment of the match into the ordinary dispersed contexts of daily (UPA) life.

Finally, the football-loving priest faces the challenge of responding to and praying through the darker side of the 'Beautiful Game'. We have noted how readily football achieves an unhealthy priority in many people's lives. It is a sad thing to encounter a person so obsessed with the sport (or, more likely, with one particular football club) that it has become their god. The experience is all the more sad because it happens often. It is one of the more easily identified idolatries of our age, and in responding to it the football-loving priest may find a helpful template in the response of St Paul to the idolatry of the Athenians, as Luke describes it in Acts 17: the distress he experiences is real, but is expressed as a generous affirmation that the devotion he has observed is in fact a truly spiritual impulse, misdirected.

Again, we have noted that in the grossly exaggerated salaries paid to top-level players, the worldwide TV broadcasting packages and the merchandizing of kit far beyond the historic 'local' catchment area of a club, football exemplifies the process of globalization. The sport is subject to forces far greater than itself, and which are at work far beyond itself, illustrating the extent to which economic trends and market forces can render whole institutions, and not just single individuals, powerless. In the face of these trends, in other words, the soccer-mad priest has a specific motivation for and a specific insight into both 'praying for England' and working for social change.

Football is a challenge to the Church. But the challenge is not 'Why can't church be more like football?' It's 'What can church learn from football?' A Church that aspires to flourish in the poorer communities of our nation and which aspires to engage working-class men effectively will embrace the question gladly. It may even embrace the 'Beautiful Game'.

Chapter 3

Imagination

Samuel Wells

*A great deal of the priest's perceived power, particularly in neigh-
bourhoods of social disadvantage, is the sense that here is someone
who has been to university, mixed with the people who run things,
and knows a lot. Knowing a lot about 'the system' and knowing a lot
about God easily blend into one another. This chapter is an account
of the transformation that can take place when worship and teaching cease to prize those who know a lot, and instead make space and
privilege for those who are prepared to open their imaginations to
God. Here the priest is not the conveyor of information but the
teasing and reassuring giver of permission and questioner of false
limitations. Those who may be judged primarily for what they are
not – children, the elderly, those with disabilities, those with low
incomes – find treasured places in such a community, so long as they
are prepared to respond ingenuously and with wonder. Those who
come to the Church for a reinforcement of their social or academic
power are likely to get a surprise.*

I wonder

Sunday morning. Out of conviction or resolution, out of habit or
a desire for a change, people assemble under the roof of a local
church. They make themselves at home: for some, this means
taking off coats, spreading themselves, and thus assigning their

territory for the next hour or so; for others, it means seeking familiar faces, exchanging words of camaraderie or concern, establishing touch and tenderness, and belonging. For newcomers, it may mean searching for familiarity, affirmation, reassurance. Those most familiar to this pattern of life are of course busy – lighting candles, setting out musical requirements, rustling vestments, maintaining a behind-the-scenes importance, ensuring all is well.

One way or another, the meeting begins. And whether in timely word or familiar text, in rousing song or simple reminder, people realize that God is among them. For some, the mundane humanity of the rest of the congregation is more of an obstacle than a stimulus to faith. Yawns, coughs and frowns are bodily reminders that concentration is elusive and the body of Christ is made up of the all-too-human. Closed eyes and rousing crescendos seek to restore a higher level of contemplation and divine encounter. For others, the earthy humanity of a regular congregation is the embodiment of hope, a location of belonging, a fleeting experience of warmth, order and enduring relationship. Such liturgical form as exists may seem a small price to pay for the rewards of personal exchange, the sharing of news, the building of trust, the prospect of coffee.

Perhaps some words of confession or a sharing of verbal or enacted reconciliation mark the significance of God's presence, and the fact that it is not to be taken for granted; perhaps some words or a song of praise gesture to God's glory and gracious and costly mercy. Perhaps some silence, if silence is possible, defines the company as a body of people fundamentally waiting on God. The first part of a conventional service has been completed: a host of diverse individuals has been gathered together, has become one body, has repented and been forgiven, and has celebrated its new identity. It has become a people ready to hear what God has to say to them. And now, now is the time when the gathered congregation expects God to speak. This is the time conventionally set aside for the reading of scripture. The disciples felt their hearts on fire as Jesus talked with them and explained the scriptures to them; just so the congregation hopes to discover and meet and be transformed as God talks with them and explains his will in Jesus to them.

But imagine that on this occasion the one telling the story never looks at the congregation, focusing instead intently on a small area just in front of her. If the congregation is small and the seating flexible, she may be kneeling on the floor to tell the story; if the congregation is larger and in pews, she may be presenting the story on a small table, having already invited the congregation to adjust their posture and location to wherever best helps them see and hear what is about to take place. The storyteller brings a story out of a box, piece by piece. Small wooden figures represent the characters, stretches of felt or textured material portray the lake, sea or path; perhaps a sand tray becomes the desert, small stones an altar, a specially crafted wooden skyline Jerusalem. The storyteller treasures the figures, cherishes them as the channels through which the precious story is made visible, the hallowed name made known. When God speaks, an open palm hovers face down over the place or person; when a poignant moment arises, the wooden figure is held tenderly in the two hands of the storyteller.

Imagine that the theme is Isaiah, and the story goes something like this.

God had a special people. They were slaves in the land of Egypt and God brought them out of slavery and took them to a new land. It took them a long time to discover who they were and who God wanted them to be. Eventually God brought them into the land he had prepared for them, and they knew they were coming home. After many years they built a special city there, and the city had walls, and the city had a special place to be close to God, called the Temple. But the people began to forget their story, and forget their God. They became more and more like other peoples. God sent prophets to warn them but they took little notice. One day their city was besieged, the walls toppled, and the Temple overrun. Many of the people were taken hundreds of miles away to another city. They were in exile. God told them not just to be sad. God told them to work hard in that city, not just for themselves but for everyone there. And they began to realize that their God wasn't just their God, but was the God of the whole world. They discovered that God could bring glory out of shame and beauty out of suffering – in fact that God could suffer too. And one day there was a new emperor. And he told them they could go home. So many of them set out back on the journey their parents and grandparents had made before them. And they came home. They rebuilt their city, and its walls. They even rebuilt the Temple. It was a new time. But some didn't return. Some stayed in the place they had called exile. Because God was there too.

Imagine this narrative being told as the storyteller traced the journey from Egypt, to the wilderness, to the Promised Land, and then gently built Jerusalem and its walls and Temple and populated it with wooden figures. Then the wooden figures would leave the destroyed city and set out on a journey to Babylon, a place that emerges as they draw near it. And behind them would fall a metal chain, a symbol of exile. To everyone's surprise the hovering hand signifying God's nearness would appear while the figures were in Babylon. And then eventually many of the figures would make the journey back and the walls and Temple would arise again. If the surface on which the wooden figures made their journeys were sand, then the echoes of earlier desert journeys made in a similar direction to the returning exiles might resonate with the congregation: journeys by Abraham, by Isaac, and by Jacob. The inching sound of wooden figures trudging across sand might evoke its own stories in the imagination of the congregation.

And when the story is over, there is a moment of quiet. And then the storyteller looks up at the congregation, and says, 'I wonder.' She proceeds to wonder out loud about the story just told. She begins simply. 'I wonder what part of this story you liked the best.' 'I wonder what part was the most important part.' 'I wonder what part was about you.' 'I wonder what part we could take out and still have all the story we need.' Such wonderings elicit personal engagement, identification and discomfort. Some may offer simple responses: 'I liked the sand.' 'I liked it that God brought them back.' Others may offer more reflection: 'The important part was when they discovered God didn't belong to them.' 'The important part was realizing that it wasn't just them suffering – God was too.' Others may disclose wisdom very close to home: 'I'm not sure I know where home is any more.' 'I've decided to stop sulking about my family break-up and try to make my life a blessing for those I now spend my time with.' Others may offer challenges. 'How about if we took away the Temple the second time? Or the city walls? Doesn't there have to be some sign that they learnt something in exile?'

If there is time, and the congregation has the engagement and enthusiasm to go further, there may be opportunity for more pro-found wondering. 'I wonder what it would have taken for them to remember their story and listen to God.' 'I wonder if the other people who lived in Babylon understood anything about this God who was God of everyone.' 'I wonder if when they came back they got back everything they'd lost.' 'I wonder if there are some things they would never have had had they not been into exile.' 'I wonder when they were closest to God – before they left, while they were away, or after they came back.' 'I wonder where our congregation is in relation to these three places.'

It may be that there is plenty of time, and if so, members of the congregation may continue to explore the story in groups, in pairs, or alone, with word or craft or creative arts. And then the wondering is over. It is time for the storyteller to replace each figure in the box. As she does so, she treasures each item – walls, figures, chain. And she prays as she does so, turning the wonderings into intercessions. 'We offer you the walls, and reflect on the walls we and others set up, against you, against one another, against our true callings . . . We offer you those who made the long journey back, recalling all refugees who long to return home . . . And we recall all those who stayed . . . We offer you the distant city, remembering the people of that city and the civil war taking place around that city today.' And then the congregation resumes a more conventional posture, and the meeting continues, and there is bread broken and wine poured, a feast in remembrance and anticipation, another enactment that is also a discovery, another way in which tangible signs disclose wonder and engagement. And finally there is blessing and a renewal of mission; and departure.

Radical discernment

In what follows I draw out some of the significance of this way of encountering the word of God.

The method of storytelling and wondering that I have here described broadly follows the catechetical approach of 'Godly Play', a Montessori-based children's curriculum devised by Jerome Berryman. Berryman is following in the footsteps of Sofia Cavalletti, an Italian who has sought to bring the Montessori tradition into harmony with the trajectory for the Roman Catholic Church set by the Second Vatican Council. Cavalletti's ethos is set out in her book *The Religious Potential of the Child* and is embodied in her children's programme known as the Catechesis of the Good Shepherd. Jerome Berryman, originally a Presbyterian, latterly an Episcopalian priest, has developed this programme and focused it more on a group of children than an individual child, more explicitly based around a eucharistic shape, and generally more accessible and adaptable to liturgically formed Protestants.

I first encountered these programmes when I was the vicar of a parish in a neighbourhood experiencing significant social disadvantage. I was leading worship for a congregation many of whom could read but for whom in general reading was an activity that reminded them of their low social standing. Of those who could and did read for pleasure, many were looking for forms of worship that were sustainable in a context where unsettled children would often wander in and out in the course of a service, sometimes seeking attention in quite distressing ways. There being little discernible enthusiasm for running a Sunday School during the main act of worship, services were generally all-age. I therefore took to exploring ways in which liturgy, sharing, education and storytelling could come together. I wanted to affirm that worship was a corporate action in which people performed some things repeatedly (and thus came to take them for granted) while remaining open to discover other things for the first time.

On one occasion in the later stages of Lent the congregation divided after the gospel reading. Some wrote words and drew images of God's passionate love for the world, and all that answered the description 'glory'. Others wrote words and drew images of God's anger and distress at human sin, and all that answered the description 'grief'. These images were then attached to a large outline of a heart – glory on the left, grief on the right. And then the presiding minister slowly tore the heart in two, saying 'God's heart is torn between glory and grief, between love for us and distress at our sin – and on the cross Jesus' heart broke in two showing us how much we mean to God.' After the service a visitor from the United States asked if we had ever heard of the Catechesis of the Good Shepherd, which was so vital to her own congregation's life. That was where our adventure with the work of Cavalletti and Berryman began.

What we discovered was a way in which children and adults complemented one another's encounter with God. The Church of England has spent a lot of time at a parish level over the last ten or more years discerning whether and how it was best for children to receive Communion prior to Confirmation. Underlying that often revealing discussion lay a neglected history. Until well into the twentieth century few supposed that children could have a genuine encounter with God: they were excluded from the liturgy until they were ready to receive. It is often remarked that the teenager was invented in the 1950s, with the rise of popular music and the extended availability of leisure time. The rise of the child as something more than the inadequate receptacle of adult wisdom dates from broadly the same period.

But what was growing, as the resources and programmes for children became more sophisticated and carefully packaged, was a fear of the child. In so many programmes a key method is to keep the child constantly on his or her toes, mentally and physically, so that interest and excitement are constantly stimulated and church never allowed to become boring. I once attended a training session for church children's workers that was full of how to keep children amused and attentive through a multi-day holiday club. A member of the audience asked, 'What do you do if a child asks a question you don't know how to answer?' 'Ah,' said the expert, 'questions: they can be a problem. The best thing is to put someone in a quiet place over in a corner, someone like the vicar, and you can send the child with a question over to them if you don't want to interrupt the session and you don't know what to say.' This exchange became a defining moment for me. It had evidently not occurred to the expert that the children might be discovering something of or about God that the adults did not already know. I realized that this was what my ministry with children was all about: not keeping them busy for fear they might become bored (with God or with me) or disruptive; but creating spaces where children could genuinely meet God, quite possibly in ways I had never imagined. So much ministry with children and young people is a noble effort to be more interesting than God, but the anxiety to keep the children's attention discloses an underlying fear that God perhaps is not so interesting after all. The key to Cavalletti's vision came when a child asked her, 'How can I meet God for myself?' Such a question puts much busy children's work in the shade.

Yet helping a child find an answer to the question, 'How can I meet God for myself?' in a sometimes troubled and frequently fractious urban neighbourhood was no sentimental matter. Some of the literature and practice of Montessori-inspired children's work can make the classroom (Cavalletti's word is 'atrium') seem like a laboratory, kept at a standard temperature and pressure. Practitioners and theorists sometimes talk of the 'innate spirituality' of the child. Ten years in ministry in urban priority areas left me somewhat agnostic on the innate spirituality of children. One simply learns always to be hopeful, seldom to be shocked, and never to take anything for granted. I sensed I was not looking for a quality or disposition deep within the essence of the child, but instead seeking to facilitate and affirm an emerging relationship between the child and God. Rather than isolate the child into an environment in which children could be alone with their spirituality, the worship of that parish church concentrated on aerating opportunities for people of every decade of human life to explore and discover wisdom and insight.

And this, it emerged, was quite unusual. The separation, generations ago, had been cerebral: children in church were to be seldom seen and never heard. Their role was to be inadequate recipients, only. The separation today is legal: children are taught to see adults as strangers and strangers as potential threats. There are few places outside the family where children and adults relate easily together, and such places – sports teams, after-school interest groups, uniformed organizations – are increasingly coming to resemble statutory schools in the regulatory requirements and the atmosphere of professionalized relationships. The kind of interaction offered by this kind of worship – cross-generational, in which acquaintances discuss matters of substance, with people of differing abilities and a variety of social class, race and status, a context that makes the difference between adults and children much less striking, in a relationship of mutual upbuilding – this is very unusual, almost unique in contemporary social engagement.

Children in general tend to wonder quite as well as adults – often better. The first 'Godly Play' presentation ever presented in the small congregation described above was the account of the miraculous catch of fish in Luke 5. On the shore were the fishermen. On the boat was Jesus, teaching so many new things and so many true things that those on the shore wanted to know more of who he was and where he was going and whether they could come too. Then the fishermen put out to sea one more time, even though they were tired. And they dragged in their net, now full of fish, almost bursting at the seams. 'I wonder where you are in this story' asked the storyteller. 'I wonder whether you are on the boat with the disciples or on the shore with Jesus.' In one eight-year-old's mind there was no doubt. 'I'm in the net with all the fish because the fish are like all the thoughts that jumble in my head on my way to school' she said.

Not only did the children inspire the adults to wonder; the entry into the shared world of the imagination and fostered mutual understanding initiated healing. There was one child whose attention deficit and hyperactivity disorder made him a constant thorn in the side of those seeking ordered activity in the church and elsewhere. Few precious items went unbroken, few special occasions went undisturbed, few walls – even the steep roof of the church – went unclimbed. One day he sauntered into the church while the congregation was beginning to explore the story of the anointing at Bethany. The rapt attention of everyone on the story drew him in and caused him to be uncharacteristically still. The story was told of how perfume was poured out, a head was wiped, the neglect of the poor was lamented, and an unnamed woman was praised. The congregation pondered. 'I wonder what it was like for the disciples when Jesus praised this woman who had just walked in from the street.' And again, 'I wonder if doing a beautiful thing is sometimes more important than simply giving money.' And then, 'I wonder what it's like to know that someone you care about very much is going to die and there's nothing you can do about it.' At this point the child who had come in and joined the discernment spoke up. 'My aunt died last January. She told us she was going to die. My uncle went mental.' He turned from being a scourge of the congregation to a spokesman of Jesus' passion. He resumed, subsequently, his role as scourge, but he had become, briefly, part of the discovery of the story, a carrier of revelation.

Over time that congregation developed two special rooms in its church building. Behind the main worship area there was created a children's worship area, rather like the atrium proposed by Sofia Cavalletti. This was the children's special place, and signs indicated that adults were only permitted to enter that space when accompanied by a child. Hence the space was kept locked when not being used by the children. Around this space were all the materials used to tell and respond to the many stories, and all the liturgical elements such as an altar and a chalice and seasonal colours that reflected the way the church embodied the story in worship. To one side of the main worship area was a second room, an adults' prayer room. This again had many liturgical elements, including an icon and significant artistic displays, together with an altar and candles and prayer stools. This was also kept locked, and children were only permitted to enter this space when accompanied by an adult. The main worship area was used not just for worship but also for dance classes, a youth club and public meetings. It was an *agora* – a Roman marketplace. It was the place where the children and the adults came together to worship, and gave each other hospitality. Giving the two age groups their own space heightened appreciation for liturgy among people many of whom did not have conventionally ordered lives. Each room had a sense of 'how we do things in here'. Each room was a place for discovering the word and sharing in the sacrament. Liturgy was simply 'the way we do things in here'. I do not recall the word 'liturgy' even being used. But almost everyone had a strong sense of 'the way we do things in here' – and why.

If the gap between adults and children is a subtle but significant one, so is the gap between worship and teaching. The period between the day the visitor from the USA said 'Have you ever heard of the Catechesis of the Good Shepherd?' and the day the boat, the fishing net and the Sea of Galilee first came out of the box was an interval of about two years. During those two years the congregation experienced an exhilarating and traumatic upheaval. The Sunday School increased in size from eight to 60 in about 12 months. These were all children who came without their parents. The ministry of a young children's worker who lived locally, was a regular presence in local schools, and ran children's clubs at the church and in the schools, was the very significant factor. Most congregations yearn for their children's work to grow so rapidly: few would be prepared for the strain that such growth would put on the existing leadership and structure of church life. Those who had taken a step away from children's ministry a year or two earlier, feeling they had no more to give, were now pressed back into service. As the numbers coming and the challenges they brought with them grew, each of the leaders fell back on their first principles. The leaders were divided three ways. One group, inspired by the charismatic children's worker, saw the central role as evangelism, which in this case was largely a matter of giving the children a good experience to go home with that encouraged them to return. This created a dynamic reminiscent of the sorcerer's apprentice – a growing number of children, with a diminishing degree of order or integration into any pattern of church life. Another group, overwhelmed with the number of children whose knowledge of the Christian tradition was wafer thin, favoured education. Here, however, there was a split between those who trusted the time-honoured approach of communicating 'Bible stories' and those who were so troubled by the manners and morale of many of the children that they were more inclined to teach simple life skills and mutual respect. I found I was in a group pretty much on my own, hoping to translate every event into worship, because I believed worship brought the restless heart to rest in God, that here the children would discover a desire deeper than all others.

The strain of this period took its toll on some of those most closely involved in the work. When things settled down, the children who had come for entertainment were largely gone, and the numbers returned to a sustainable level, given the size of the adult congregation. That was the moment when we started to share scripture stories 'from the box' and with wondering. It turned out that this form of service largely satisfied all three desires. Those concerned with reaching children in the neighbourhood found that many such children did still appear, only they came expecting less to be given something than to give something themselves. Those concerned with communicating a knowledge of Bible stories were more than happy that such stories were an integral part of the church's worship – although they began to discover the stories anew themselves in unexpected ways. And I was content that we had brought this about by keeping worship and its community and character-forming quality at the centre of our congregational life.

It was at this point, for the first time in my period as the incumbent, that people began to notice not the empty seats but the quality of what was happening among the people actually there. For a long time, significant voices in the congregation had been focused on what might be possible if one day we had more people. Well, for a year or so we did have more people and it turned out very little was possible. Again through accident rather than design, we went back to having fewer people. Then one day someone said, 'You know, if we had more people, we couldn't do some of the things we do.' And it was undoubtedly so. What we were doing was hearing God's voice in the words of one another, being silent together while paying rapt attention to the scriptural story, cherishing the insights of youth and the ages, and weighing all up in a process of communal discernment.

It was not simply a matter of telling the story. One year New Year coincided with a celebration of the Epiphany. This time the story of the three magi and the flight to Egypt was read conventionally, rather than coming out of a box. What did come out of a box were three ribbons. One marked a journey from Nazareth to Bethlehem. Another marked a journey from Bethlehem to Egypt. A third marked a journey from Egypt to Nazareth. Nazareth marked a place of nurture, Bethlehem a place of danger, and Egypt a place of escape. Together they formed a triangle. Each person had a trio of coloured adhesive dots. One colour marked where they had been on the triangle in the course of the last year. A second colour marked where they expected to be in the year to come. A third marked where they imagined the congregation would be in the year to come. The assortment of dots made a pattern on the triangle. And then the congregation pondered. 'I wonder what is a good place on this triangle to be,' said one voice. 'I wonder how the congregation is going to be over here if all its people are expecting to be over there,' said another. 'I wonder if all the dots are equally important,' said a third. This was an unforgettable experience of community formation and shared imagination shaped by the scriptural story.

This style of engaging the word and the tradition brought together worship and education and old and young. It also elided the distinction between the newcomer and the expert. Congregations can very easily become pecking orders, in which those who associate scriptural knowledge with holiness assign to themselves the highest seats at the right hand of the power. But wondering is not like this. It is not about the expert storyteller mesmerizing the congregation with her knowledge or the learned scholar humiliating the congregation with their ignorance. Wondering does not test knowledge. A sentence that begins 'I wonder' does not have a question mark at the end. Wondering stretches the imagination, challenges compassion, provokes empathy, trains perception. The newcomer may bring as much or more to this exercise of listening and discerning as the most established regular.

Some of my most memorable experiences with this kind of scriptural exploration have come in prisons. Some of those in prison are longing to get back to a place of childlike discovery – to get back in time to a simpler condition of life and to get in their imaginations to a place where the prison bars do not dictate the boundaries of their lives. Other prisoners are resistant and terrified of getting back to an imaginative place where most of the damage in their lives was done, and are well aware that most of their lives has been spent running away from what happened to them as a child. On one evening 14 prisoners and some visitors from the prison fellowship sat down for an hour to talk about the Lord's Prayer. It came out of a box.

Here is the first request: 'Give us.' It's about the present. It's about offering God our fear that we won't have enough to get through today. Here's the second request. 'Forgive us.' It's about the past. It's about offering God the things we've done and the things that have been done to us and letting go of them and asking God to deal with them. Here's the third request. 'Deliver us.' It's about offering God our fear that the future will present us with challenges that are too much for us, either because we are weak or because the challenges are superhuman. Now . . . I wonder which one of these requests is the hardest to say. I wonder which one tells us the most about God. I wonder which one of these are we most keen to keep God out of.

A noticeably articulate member of the group refused to entertain the idea that he had ever been afraid. He insisted he had no need to pray the request, 'Deliver us.' It transpired that he had never known his mother, had realized from the age of four that his father was frequently paralytic with drink, and from then on had learned to take money, go to the shops by himself, and generally make himself independent of the care or concern of anyone else. Of course fear was alien to him. He had edited it out of his life in order to survive. But doing so had put him where he was. Such a discussion took me close to the heart of the gospel in a way one seldom experiences even in pastoral ministry.

A rather different experience came about on a later visit to the same prison, with a similar number of participants and members of the prison visiting fellowship. This time the story was of Jesus' crucifixion. There were three crosses, and as each cross was set up the narration went, 'No one could have wanted or imagined their life would end this way.' The pondering after the conclusion of the story dwelt on the nature of punishment and the despair of those on death row. It was time to suggest a line of thought. 'I wonder whether Jesus knew as he hung on the cross that he would be raised on the third day.' The dozen or so prisoners were pensive. They had been relating Jesus' suffering to their own experience of having been convicted and awaiting their sentence. The member of the prison fellowship was having none of it, however: 'Of course he did – he'd predicted it three times!' No more wondering for him.

A final misleading polarity reframed by this kind of communal discernment is the distinction between the scriptural world and the 'real' world. Two overdrawn sermon styles may illustrate the way this problem is often set up. On the one hand is the sermon that carefully sets a scripture passage in context, both historically and existentially, then walks through the key points in the passage, showing in many cases how each point is linked to a schema of some kind, before concluding by drawing out one or a series of applications to contemporary life. On the other hand is the sermon that is mainly concerned with identifying the human experience, process or wisdom taken up by the passage of the day. It sometimes sees a tension between human experience and the biblical witness, and occasionally questions the biblical witness on such grounds – sermons on the sacrifice of Isaac or certain views of the atonement being familiar examples. When done well, both of these approaches have much to offer the Church. However, it is easy to see that on one side are those who, convinced of Christian identity, nonetheless struggle to make that identity relevant to the society to which they speak. On the other side are those who, convinced of the obligation to be relevant, still struggle to show how that relevance is grounded in Christian identity.

Storytelling that invites the imaginative participation of the congregation has the potential to overcome this polarity between identity and relevance. It affirms Christian identity because it absorbs the listener and viewer into the world of the scripture as the 'real' world; but it affirms the experience of the congregation by inviting a wondering discovery of what it means to inhabit that new world. It is no longer a matter of how to 'apply' or 'justify' the words of revelation: it is now a prayerful but spontaneous participation in the scriptures themselves, as a character in God's story. For people living in an area of social disadvantage, discovering that they could be a character in God's story was one of the most significant gifts of all.

The power of the imagination

Mr Gradgrind knew the power of wondering.

> When she was half-a-dozen years younger, Louisa had been overheard to begin a conversation with her brother one day by saying, 'Tom, I wonder' – upon which Mr Gradgrind, who was the person overhearing, stepped forth into the light and said, 'Louisa, never wonder!'
>
> Herein lay the spring of the mechanical art and mystery of educating the reason without stooping to the cultivation of the sentiments and affections. Never wonder. By means of addition, subtraction, multiplication and division, settle everything somehow, and never wonder. 'Bring to me, says M'Choakumchild, yonder baby just able to walk, and I will engage that it shall never wonder' (Charles Dickens, *Hard Times*, Everyman, p. 48).

The Church constantly agonizes about the use and misuse of power, about participation in politics, about incorporating and affirming diversity in public life. But its most important contribution to such questions is to embody its proposals.

I lived for ten years in socially disadvantaged parts of England – for four years in the north east and for six years in west Norwich. When I began I was angry about wealth inequalities, and a lot of that anger was directed at people who had a lot of money. When I was in poorer communities I felt at peace – not just that I was spending my time with the people Jesus spent his time with, but that I was being part of the solution rather than continuing to be part of the problem.

When eventually it was time for me to leave this style of ministry, I had learned that poverty is not fundamentally about money. I discerned that there were two key dimensions to life in the areas in which I had been living. One was community. People in west Norwich in fact had many things their neighbours in the richer parts of the town didn't have. They often had extended families: rather than spending all weekend driving to see granny, granny lived in the next street, a block or two away. The children had space in which to play. Rather than have streets teeming with cars, there were relatively few cars so the streets were relatively safe for play. Rather than work hard enough to buy a house with a private yard where the children could play alone, many local people allowed their children to play with anyone who came along, and were seldom let down. The second key element was imagination. Imagination essentially means being able to conceive of a world different from this one. Imagination is fostered through cosmopolitan cultures, travel, the reading of literature, music and opportunities to participate in visual and dramatic arts. These were not extensive in west Norwich.

I concluded that what was required was something to do (imagination) and someone to do it with (community). The former included education, entrepreneurship, confidence and resilience; the latter involved friendship, financial support and cultural understanding. If you have something to do and someone to do it with, you are not really poor, even if you don't have much money. If you lack either of these things, then you can have a large amount of money but your life is impoverished. I learned this while I was helping to lead a government-sponsored community-led social and economic regeneration programme which brought £35 million to the neighbourhood over ten years. We actually found it difficult to spend some of the money, because there were surprisingly few instances where simple lack of money was the problem. The problems were about imagination and community.

After this I stopped being so angry about wealth inequalities. I started to see that the role of the Church was to be a community of imagination that demonstrated the imaginative possibilities of social relations not previously thought possible. Rather than get cross with rich people, who I found were as powerless to make things better as those with much less money, I concentrated on making churches into communities of imagination. And then for the first time I began to imagine how I might serve people who were not economically poor – but were nonetheless seeking the imagination and community that the Church and the gospel have at their heart. And I have never seen that hospitable, inclusive, imaginative politics more engagingly displayed than in the practice of communal wondering, gathered around God's story.

*   *   *

Bibliographical Note

Those wishing to explore God's story through wondering may wish to read Sofia Cavalletti, *The Religious Potential of the Child: Experiencing Scripture and Liturgy with Young Children* (translated by Julie M. Coulter, Liturgy Training Publications, 1988) and Jerome Berryman, *The Complete Guide to Godly Play, Volume One: How to Lead Godly Play Lessons* (Living the Good News, 2002). I am grateful to Rebecca Nye for early conversations around 'Godly Play', to Brenda Huddleston for introducing me to prison ministry, and to Stuart Warren for pointing out the role of wondering in Charles Dickens.

Chapter 4

Presence

Edmund Newey

Perhaps the place where more people encounter a priest than in other ways is through the 'occasional' offices of baptism and marriage, and, most of all, through funeral ministry. It is very common for those new to ministry to be overwhelmed more than anything else by the quantity and quality of their encounters with families at the time of death. This chapter is a sustained engagement with what a priest is trying to do and to be in the course of offering pastoral care and liturgical ministry at such times. It reflects in particular on the ambiguities of the notion of home, a particularly resonant word in relation to faith and to death. Being 'present' in the homes of those in shock and bereavement is the stuff of the parish priest's work – a duty rarely celebrated, but subtly expressing the priest's invisible role as negotiator of the boundary between life and death.

One of the great themes of recent theology has been the rediscovery that every aspect of life is potentially liturgical – that, in a phrase of Rowan Williams', the Christian life is about 'giving glory to the giver of glory'. This truth gains popular expression in Jan Struther's hymn, 'Lord of all hopefulness'. In the everyday pattern of life – waking and working and homing and sleeping, as the hymn's four verses put it – there God is to be found, served and praised. Now it would be unfair to expect one hymn to say everything, but if 'Lord of all hopefulness' has a theological defect it is perhaps this: that in its welcome stress on the worship of God in our daily routines, it misses any sense of where God might be when those routines are interrupted. The hymn resolves life's pattern into a divine harmony. Joy, faith, grace and calm, it implies, are the hallmarks of our encounter with God, but does this suggest that when those qualities are absent God is absent too? For me, this question is at its sharpest in the third verse:

> Be there at our homing,
> and give us, we pray,
> your love in our hearts, Lord,
> at the eve of the day.

The poet's choice of the word 'homing' is an attractive one. It appeals to our sense that the home is a place of solace and protection, a place where feet are put up and masks laid aside. Yet, treasured though this image may be in modern British culture, in practice the home is not always where we are most 'at home'. For many people – perhaps for most people at times of transition and stress – the metaphor and the reality do not coincide. The teenager straining at the parental leash; the 'looked-after' child who lingers after school, seeking the continuity she has lost after her parents' conviction for drug dealing; the widower, ill at ease in a house no longer made homely by the care of his wife. Each of these recent examples from the parish in which I serve could be multiplied across the country.

I am here seeking to explore the instance of this phenomenon of 'domestic homelessness' that is probably most common: the experience of bereavement. My aim is not to replicate the many excellent clinical studies of grief and mourning, but to reflect on what is at stake more generally in the Church's work with the bereaved. Tracing the stages of this rewarding ministry, I seek to show how thoroughly liturgical it is. The liturgy may be as inconspicuous as a prayer said quietly over a cup of tea, but in accompanying people through those traumatic passages of life when the domestic sphere is invaded by grief and loss, the priest is carrying out a task that is at the very heart of the Church's ministry. Just as Christ gave glory to the giver of glory at all times and in all places – and supremely in the abandonment and exaltation of the cross – so can his disciples, learning to live liturgically, 'at home' with God in life's shocks as well as in its routines.

The home

Discussing the question of what constitutes a home, the literary historian Robert Harrison has written this: 'For as long as we think of our houses . . . as merely places in which to live, and not as places in which to die, those houses . . . can never become homes or take their stand within the limits of containment from which all shelter and placehood ultimately derive.' In support of this contention, he argues that the first permanent structures made by human beings were burial mounds. The origins of architecture lay, he believes, in the impetus to provide shelter not for the living but for the deceased: human beings housed their dead before they housed themselves. To contemporary ears, Harrison's suggestion is bound to seem implausible. The places in which we take leave of our dead today – our cemeteries and crematoria – are almost invariably on the margins of our everyday habitat; those who visit them are regarded with unease or, at best, sympathy. Both in our imaginations and usually in practice, we keep the home and the grave at a safe remove one from the other, and to suggest that they are somehow interdependent will appear scandalous. Yet, if Harrison is correct, in enforcing such a rigorous demarcation between the places where we house our dead and the places where we house ourselves, we are threatening, not protecting, our treasured sense of the home. Could it be that the home is only to be found through coming up against Harrison's 'limits of containment', through the encounter with death and loss?

The burden of Harrison's argument is that, on the traditional understanding, the home was the place where two realms interpenetrated – that of the dead under the earth and that of the living above it. Of course, burials often took place outside the immediate space of the home, but the point he emphasizes is the imaginative proximity between the two realms. Drawing on the analogy proposed by Giambattista Vico, that '*humanitas* in Latin comes first and properly from *humando*, burying', he suggests that it is through a proper engagement with 'death as the very condition and ground of life', that the human race is able to endow its life with meaning and purpose: 'The dead are our guardians. We give them a future, so that they may give us a past.' As the place at once of birth and death, of celebration and mourning, the home formed the ligature between past, present and future. It was precisely the co-existence of these apparently conflicting spheres that made the house into a home.

Harrison writes as a literary scholar and disavows any religious competence. Nonetheless, both theologically and pastorally, his proposals are remarkably suggestive. In Christian terms, what they omit is simply a liturgical application: an account of the ways in which the process of properly coming to terms with death can also be the opening to an encounter with the transcendence and immanence of God. What Harrison terms the 'pedagogy of grief', by which we learn to be 'at home' with the dead and with the living, can also be the pedagogy of hope, by which we await a new 'home' in God. Such a learning process is inherently liturgical, liturgy being defined in the broadest terms as the encounter between God and humanity writ large. With Harrison's insights as its starting point, this chapter looks at the Church's funeral ministry through the liturgical lens of the human desire to be 'at home' – with oneself, with one's departed loved ones, and with God.

In what follows I begin by reflecting on the particular dynamic that characterizes the presence of a priest in the home of a non-churchgoer. In what is often an awkward encounter, the priest may initially be perceived as a professional spiritual emissary, sent to deal with an incident – death – that calls for help from beyond the usual channels. What is more, the priest may well see him- or herself in the same light. In this context of misunderstanding the focus needs to be on the rediscovery of common humanity in the face of death. God's presence can be recognized, even in the desolation of the here and now. In the face of death, we are still 'at home' with one another and with God.

At the funeral itself this dynamic shifts subtly. For the bereaved the awkwardness may persist or grow, as they enter an unfamiliar building, perhaps for the first time. For the priest, on the other hand, the temptation can be to feel excessively 'at home', once again to be cast in the role of professional funeral expert. The need at this stage is to recognize that in liminal places, such as churches and chapels, we are all brought into the presence of a reality that questions our very being. Whether that reality is death (for the atheist) or God (for those who entertain the possibility of faith), awe and reverence are the appropriate emotions. As the priest gestures to God's presence at the boundaries of life in our doubts, fears and questionings, he or she also points to the Christian hope of a new home in heaven, restating Christ's promise that 'where I am, there you may be also' (John 14.3).

Sometimes it is at this point that the Church's ministry will cease, but many parishes have found that, either by a system of lay visiting or through invitations to a monthly requiem or an annual All Souls' Day service, the bereaved welcome further contact. I have chosen to focus on the last of these. However well the visit and the funeral may have communicated something of the reality of God's immanence (*here*) and transcendence (*there*), all too often the ensuing months, rather than allowing the time and space for these experiences to be assimilated, instead leave them half-forgotten, associated with an episode that is left behind as the bereaved 'get on with their lives'. It is into this half-forgetfulness that the All Souls' liturgy can speak. Its purpose, some months after the death, is to rekindle these encounters with God – in the now and the not yet – and open them up to one another by the renewing gift of liturgy.

Through each of these three stages of ministry with the bereaved, the Church's ministry is marked by a liturgical hospitality that helps people learn to be 'at home' with themselves, with their bereavement and with God: meeting them where they are, allowing them to relate to their past and helping them to hope in what is yet to come. More theologically, it brings all God's people – ministers and bereaved alike – to the foot of the cross, the liturgical place *par excellence*, where the extremity of loss meets the consummation of love.

The funeral visit: 'an awkward animal'

An overlooked fact about the Church of England is that across the country, day by day, its clergy are being welcomed into the homes of people they have never met before. In 2004 just over 227,000 funerals were conducted in the Church of England and it is safe to assume that nearly all of those services were preceded by one or more visits to bereaved relatives. For many clergy, such visits are the staple of their pastoral contact with those outside the congregation, and, as such, they are an opportunity and a blessing. An opportunity because it is so rare to be invited, *specifically as a Christian minister,* into a non-churchgoing household; a blessing because, time after time, here we glimpse new expanses of the gospel we preach, revealing the activity of God's love within and outside the visible Church.

David Scott has quietly articulated the feel of a typical funeral visit in this poem:

My Bike

I prop it up, steady it,
pull my trousers out of my socks,
and knock to enter into
a death, or any other
of life's routine shocks.
'Bring it in.' I carry it like an awkward animal and
introduce it to the shoes and shopping,
where it waits.
The talk ranges
from the now, to the past, to the weather
mostly skirting eternity.
I carry it out into new air,
where it takes the strain
in the pedals. We weave between ducks
and day-outers, until it hits the garage
almost horizontal, like a laid hedge,
among bits of hose, tired footballs,
the rusty sledge. It sleeps where it falls.

(*Selected Poems*, Bloodaxe, 1998)

As a bicycling priest, I warm to this poem. For all the endless variety of the ways in which it may strike, and whether the death has been foreseen or not, the experience of bereavement is always 'an awkward animal'. Like a bicycle carried into the living space of a house, it is an intrusion, an unfamiliar visitor out of place in the domestic sphere. But if the bicycle in this poem is an image of bereavement, at a deeper level it is also a metaphor for the Church and its ministry. A bike is not always the most convenient mode of transport – I have arrived for funeral visits blue with cold in the winter, red with summer heat, once even black-handed with oil after a slipped chain! – but it is surprising how often, like the poem's invitation 'Bring it in', it breaks the ice and begins to put the conversation on a relatively natural footing.

The priest comes neither as qualified professional nor as well-meaning amateur, but as a fellow human being with particular experience of the poorly mapped territory around death. In this context, 'awkward animal' though it is, the bike stands for two vital hallmarks of the Church's ministry: vulnerability and patience. The bicycle indicates that there is someone here who is willing to expend personal energy, to take time, to be at home with those who may be feeling very far from 'at home'. Often the priest's visit, following hard on that of the ambulance or the undertakers' van, is part of the invasion of the privacy of the home first by loss and then by the public sphere that attends it. In this context of alien-ation, where dis-ease has intruded into the home, the priest's first duty is simply to help the bereaved family to begin to rediscover a sense of ease: first with him or her personally; but more impor-tantly with their loss and with the often very alien environment of the Church with which the funeral will confront them. The challenge is to offer and receive Christ's hospitality, to help the bereaved re-imagine themselves in the new context of their loss.

Once over the threshold, the awkwardness, though tamed, is unlikely to dissipate immediately.

> The talk ranges
> from the now, to the past, to the weather
> mostly skirting eternity

writes David Scott, capturing beautifully the ways in which the question mark of God hangs, recognized but unarticulated, over so much of the conversation. For the Christian, the natural impulse is to offer the situation to God in prayer, yet it can be astonishingly difficult to find appropriate ways to do so in a home where spoken prayer is unknown. Jarring insensitivity is the last thing the circumstances require, and the temptation is often strong to leave the prayer implicit: just a parting 'God bless', or a silent petition while the cup of tea is being prepared.

The most reliable solution to this dilemma that I have found is to explore with the assembled company what resources for prayer they already possess. The raw materials of liturgy can be found even in the most unexpected places, and, discussing a favourite reading or hymn or song, almost invariably the basis of a prayer is already there. This is most obviously the case with popular funeral hymns, such as 'O love that wilt not let me go' or 'Abide with me'. Once they have been discussed with the family, these can readily be adapted and incorporated into an improvized prayer. And, even in the sort of home where any sort of collective Christian memory seems absent, relatively fertile ground may still be found in the chosen CD. From different ends of the generational spectrum, Vera Lynn singing 'We'll meet again' and Coldplay's 'Fix you', are examples of the sort of 'secular' thread from which a prayer may be spun.

Underlying all of this, my purpose as a priest is to help the grieving relatives recognize that, despite the displacement of their loss, *here and now* is where they are still at home, and also where God is at home with them. 'Lord, it is good for us to be *here*' (Mark 9.5 and parallels), says Peter, dazed and disorientated to the transfigured Christ. Those are words that I try to keep, unspoken, at the back of my mind at every funeral visit. However inappropriate the adjective 'good' may seem in the context of grief and loss, even at this early stage of bereavement the need remains to recognize the inevitability of death – the mortality that marks all creation. It is not in spite of this inevitability, but because of it, that bereavement is one of the key places where God's blessing is to be sought and found: 'The Lord gave, and the Lord has taken away; blessed be the name of the Lord' (Job 1.21b); or, in a well-known prayer that speaks to many in the shadow of death:

God be in my head, and in my understanding;
God be in my eyes, and in my looking;
God be in my mouth, and in my speaking;
God be in my heart, and in my thinking;
God be at my end, and at my departing.
Amen.

Our heavenly home: there and not yet

Once the funeral visit is over, apart from the occasional brief telephone call, the next encounter between priest and mourners is likely to be outside the church or (crematorium or cemetery) chapel. On the day of the funeral the bereaved will be required to enter an unfamiliar place, but the unease felt on entering a church or chapel is best engaged with constructively. Though we may regret our culture's marginalization of death, there is a paradoxical sense in which, precisely as marginal and unfamiliar, churches and chapels are fitting places for the territory surrounding death. To the extent that they point beyond themselves, such buildings have the potential to gesture, however inchoately, to the transcendence of God and the hope of a new home in heaven. Thus, whereas the visit offers the opportunity to explore the presence of God in the *here and now* of the home, the funeral itself is the chance to explore the other mode of divine presence, God's transcendence in the *there and not yet*. It is not coincidental that the most popular funeral reading is from John 14, containing Jesus' reassurances: 'in my Father's house there are many dwelling places', and 'where I am, there you may be also'. In the often unfamiliar 'sacred space' of a church, an appropriate liturgy can offer at least some pointers to the whereabouts of that hoped-for heavenly home.

The sensitivity of the moment of entry into the church has been well recognized by the compilers of the *Common Worship* order. One of the great advantages of the new service is that, unlike its predecessor in the *Alternative Service Book*, it does not ask of the mourners a clear profession of faith at its very opening. The 1980 service began with a congregational affirmation of faith that, especially at this stage in the liturgy, simply asked too much of the average mourner. The *Common Worship* order does not lose this note of confident hope, but allows it to be voiced by the minister – here acting vicariously, rather in the way outlined by Grace Davie:

We meet in the name of Jesus Christ,
who died and was raised to the glory of God the Father.
Grace and mercy be with you.
All   And also with you.

These words of greeting, recollection and hope are then usually followed by another liturgical exchange, this time not with the priest but with God, in the form of the prayers of penitence. Having prompted the congregation to acknowledge the failures of communication that are part of all relationships severed by death, the wording I generally follow is this:

As children of a loving heavenly Father,
Let us ask his forgiveness,
for he is gentle and full of compassion.

Silence is kept.

Remember, Lord, your compassion and love,
for they are everlasting.
Lord, have mercy.
All   Lord, have mercy.

Remember not my sins or my transgressions, O Lord,
but think on me in your goodness,
according to your steadfast love.
Christ, have mercy.
All   Christ, have mercy.

O keep my soul and deliver me;
let me not be put to shame,
for I have put my trust in you.
Lord, have mercy.
All   Lord, have mercy.

May God our Father forgive us our sins
and bring us to the eternal joy of his kingdom,
where dust and ashes have no dominion.
All   Amen.

Clergy are sometimes wary of encouraging too much vicarious transferral in worship, but these words, adapted from Psalm 25, seem to me to strike a fine balance. At this, perhaps the most sensitive moment of the service before the prayer of commendation, these opening dialogues – between priest and congregation, and between them both and God – allow the congregation a voice in the liturgy, without asking too much too soon in terms of commitment. The two exchanges gently encourage the mourners to enter into the mode of liturgy, where finite humanity dares to address the infinity of God.

Space does not permit me to discuss the full shape of a funeral service, but the overall movement needs to be from grief, through remembrance, to hope. At many funerals this is relatively easily achieved. Especially in the cases of those who have died old and full of years, the threefold pattern of thanksgiving for the past, remembering in the present and hoping for the future comes relatively naturally. The most difficult funerals from this point of view tend to be those of children or young people, especially where the end has not been foreseen. Nonetheless, by God's grace, even such tragic occasions can allow the liturgical encounter between humanity and God to reach with its healing touch many who are normally beyond its scope. For this reason I take as an example the funeral of 'Paul', a young man in his twenties, who had taken his own life and, many hours later, had been found dead in his bedsit by his girlfriend.

In such a case it is generally not one but several visits that are required in the run-up to the funeral, especially when, as here, family tensions meant that not all the mourners were ready to gather in the same room. Two things were clear from early on: first that the church would be full to overflowing – the young man had been very popular; and second that the majority of the congregation would not have been inside a church since their childhood. Given these realities, my priority for the funeral was to enable the mourners to give voice to what they were going through, but not simply by buying into the prevailing culture that encourages public displays of emotion. The service needed to help the mourners 'come up for air' in the present, acknowledging all that they had collectively been through, and to look ahead to the future; or, in the terms I have been using, to meet God's grace both in the *now* and the *not yet*.

Perhaps the most obvious deficiency at many young people's funerals is the failure to find any means of voicing emotion corporately. Listening to tributes and favourite pieces of music has great value, but there is also a need for some form of communal expression of feeling. On one memorable occasion this lack was so strong that, after an impassioned tribute from a friend, some of the deceased's drinking partners broke into a football-style chorus, chanting his name: 'Wayne-o, Wayne-o, Wayne-o'. I felt what they were trying to express, but equally it was clear that their behaviour was distressing many of the other mourners, and a bit of uncharacteristic assertion from the lectern was needed to restore order! With this episode in mind, I was determined at Paul's funeral to find a hymn or song with which all could at least try to join in. Traditionally, humans have valued singing as the best means of giving controlled expression to grief. 'Great passions [are vented] by breaking into song,' said Giambattista Vico, rehearsing an ancient belief. Yet, in a culture where the odd sing-along chorus at a karaoke night is the nearest many come to public singing, Vico's observation may seem outdated. Taking a 'focus group' of the young man's friends, suggestion after suggestion met with little response. Even those old stand-bys 'Morning has broken' and 'All things bright and beautiful' seemed to be unfamiliar to many. Then somebody spoke up and said that he remembered one song that they used to sing at school: something about 'oil in my lamp'. A quick rendition of the chorus 'Sing hosanna, sing hosanna, sing hosanna to the King of kings!' later, and we all knew we had hit upon the answer. Content-wise, it may not have been the most obvious funeral hymn, but on recognition-factor alone it won.

On the day of the funeral the church started filling up from 40 minutes before the service, and with each new arrival the emotional pitch rose. As so often, it was music that helped to channel some of this energy. The organ music before the service seemed to have little effect, but, on entering the church with the coffin, the chosen track (Robbie Williams singing 'Let me entertain you') set off a palpable wave of feeling. It was at this point that, thanks to the music, the congregation at last began to relax. Certainly they were not feeling 'at home', but they were at least now aware of their surroundings and of what had brought them into this strange building. During the course of the service, two further tracks were played, one between the readings, and one after the address. This profusion of music stemmed from the need to cater for the choices of each constituency among the mourners, but with each song that was played some of the emotional power of the first piece was being dissipated. It seemed to me that we were heading into the territory of self-indulgence, as the music became less of a shared experience and returned more to its conventional cultural role as entertainment, distraction or background noise.

After the intercessions, it was into this atmosphere of gradually diffusing attentiveness – to the deceased, to the present moment, and, for some at least, to God – that the chosen hymn had to speak. As the congregation turned a page in the Order of Service and realized that they were about to be asked to sing, the air of reluctance was apparent. Having half-expected this, I described the effect the song had had on the small group of Paul's friends. 'That was Paul,' one of them had said, as he described how Paul brought a smile to the faces of everyone he met: he had been like the oil that kept their lamps burning. I suggested that in singing together we were showing our solidarity with Paul and could, if we wished, use the song as a prayer for him. As the organ struck up, I had no idea whether anyone would join in, but from the first 'Give' to the last 'King!' the church was filled with some of the most heartfelt singing I have heard. What it lacked in quality was made up for by volume and intensity. 'Everyone has the voice of an apprentice angel,' says John Bell of the Iona community, and the blending of thanksgiving, sorrow and hope was one of the most powerful liturgical moments I have experienced, lighting up the whole of the service that surrounded it.

Liturgy

There are, of course, obvious limitations to the liturgy the Church can offer at a funeral. At a crematorium the gentle whir of the remotely closed curtains, partially masked by the playing of an electronic organ, is the nearest we are likely to come to a liturgical action. Partly for this reason, in recent years, many parishes have begun the practice of inviting back the families of those who have died during the previous year to an All Souls' Day service in early November. In this final section I shall look at the ways in which such services can begin to open broken hearts to the reality of God, precisely by offering something more full-bloodedly liturgical than the majority of people may ever have come across.

The work of the contemporary French theologian, Jean-Yves Lacoste, has shed illuminating theoretical light on this. The surprising central contention of his description of liturgy is that it is not a natural human phenomenon. By this he does not mean that liturgy is not widely – perhaps universally – practised, but that, whenever a liturgical act is performed, it brings into question human self-sufficiency. This is perhaps best seen by comparing liturgy with play. Just as time spent in play is actually not so much 'spent' as simply lived, so the time and place of liturgy elude the utilitarian calculations of everyday existence. Of course both liturgy and play may be co-opted and corrupted – I may 'play' football for a living or plan a new church service to attract wealthier worshippers and pay the parish share – but in essence they escape such logic by being inherently purposeless. And in this they share in the purposelessness of God: as Lacoste says, 'God is purposeless, not as being less than useful, but as being more than useful; not at all by deficit, but by excess.' Liturgical time, then, is simply a waiting on the present moment as the moment of *kairos*, the revelatory point of encounter with God. We might add here that *chronos* (clock time) and *kairos* (God's time) are not so dramatically opposed as is sometimes suggested; rather, they require one another because, as Michael Ramsey pointed out, we must spend many minutes in stillness to enjoy one minute of prayer.

For these reasons, in contrast to planning a funeral to bridge the gap between the familiar and the unfamiliar, I aim in the All Souls' Day liturgy for something that will be much more on the margins of most people's experience. This is not to be exclusive, but to help everyone present to see that an hour spent remembering 'those whom we love but see no longer', giving thanks for them and praying for them, is not an hour wasted, but an hour lived to the full. If this can be achieved then the All Souls' liturgy may even take us to the supreme earthly point of *kairos* itself, the foot of the cross, which is at once the place of total loss *and* the only place of hope, where God's covenant with humanity is renewed. The place where we find ourselves at last 'at home' – fully human, yet living unto God.

To flesh out some of this theory, I shall give a brief outline of the order of service I use. This is an adapted version of 'A Service of Prayers and Readings in Commemoration of the Faithful Departed' from *The Promise of his Glory*, sadly absent from the new *Common Worship: Times and Seasons* volume. Beginning in near darkness and to the accompaniment of reflective music, the liturgy begins without ceremony: just a brief greeting and introduction, a responsory and a collect. Then, as a traditional hymn such as 'Abide with me' is sung, a candle is lit beside a crucifix, icon or other image of Christ. There follow three readings. The first is Paul's great confession of faith in Romans 8.31–39, read by a member of the regular congregation who has recently experienced bereavement. This powerful assertion of Christian hope – 'Who will separate us from the love of Christ?' – would be too much for the average funeral, but it fits perfectly with the mood of All Souls' tide. For obvious pastoral reasons this should be succeeded by a reading which allows more room for the persistence of uncertainty and grief. I find this responsorial version of Psalm 42 most appropriate. Like the penitential kyrie at the funeral service, it allows the congregation to express their continuing disorientation and doubt, while entering personally into the language of liturgy:

All   My soul is athirst for God, even for the living God.

My tears have been my bread day and night,
while all day long they say to me, 'Where is now
your God?'
Why are you so full of heaviness, O my soul,
and why are you so disquieted within me?
O put your trust in God;
for I will yet give him thanks, who is the help of my
     countenance, and my God.

All   My soul is athirst for God, even for the living God.

My soul is heavy within me;
therefore I will remember you from the land of Jordan,
     and from Hermon and the hill of Mizar.
Deep calls to deep in the thunder of your waterfalls;
all your breakers and waves have gone over me.
The Lord will grant his loving-kindness in the daytime;
through the night his song will be with me,
a prayer to the God of my life.

All   My soul is athirst for God, even for the living God.

Why are you so full of heaviness, O my soul?
and why are you so disquieted within me?
O put your trust in God;
for I will yet give him thanks,
who is the help of my countenance, and my God.

All   My soul is athirst for God, even for the living God.

The final reading is Jesus' 'Bread of Life' discourse from John 6,
during which further candles are lit in the sanctuary and chancel,
though the nave is left in relative obscurity. After this sequence of
readings there follows the address, which seeks to draw out some

of the themes implicit in the liturgy, and focuses on the image of Christ before which the candle has been lit. It is best kept as brief as possible, because in the All Souls' liturgy the role normally played by the exposition of God's word in sermon and creed is taken by the commemoration of the departed. First, the names of the departed are read out, ideally by two voices; then the congregation is invited to come forward to light candles before the image of Christ, while the choir sings an anthem or a Taizé-style chant is sung; finally, after a period of silence, there follows a concluding prayer, once again shared between priest and people. Having experimented with various texts, the one I have found most appropriate is this combination of John Donne's famous prayer with the response from the Orthodox prayer for the departed found in *The Promise of His Glory*. Purists may object, but this meeting of the Eastern and Western traditions speaks powerfully with the sober inebriation of all true liturgy:

All Give rest, O Christ, to your servants with your saints, where sorrow and pain are no more, but life everlasting.

Bring us, O Lord, at our last awakening into the house and gate of heaven, to enter into that gate and dwell in that house where there shall be no darkness nor dazzling, but one equal light; no noise nor silence, but one equal music; no fears nor hopes, but one equal possession; no ends nor beginnings, but one equal eternity in the habitations of thy glory and dominion, world without end.
Amen.

All Give rest, O Christ, to your servants with your saints, where sorrow and pain are no more, but life everlasting.

'The holiness of the heart's affections'

This chapter has been written under the title of 'Presence'. Those familiar with recent continental philosophy will know that this is not a term that can be used naïvely. This is not the place to pursue the details of this debate, but it may be useful to point out that the presence referred to here is, above all, that of the present moment. The priest in his or her pastoral work with the bereaved is a minister of the present moment. In the face of the countless ways we defer the present and distract ourselves from its demands and blessings, the priest reminds (and is reminded) that the present is the only point in time where we can be 'at home' with ourselves, and, by the same token, the only time when God is 'at home' with us. It is only in the present that 'life everlasting' is encountered.

As we have seen, there is much in our contemporary culture that militates against a proper engagement with the reality of death. The attractions of nostalgic lament and shallow emotion, and the deeper denial of which they are often the masks, are strong. Yet the surest remedy for the displacement and alienation – the 'homelessness' – of grief is to be drawn deeper into the reality of the present. Here the Church has much to offer. As we engage liturgically with the death of those to whom we have been close, in Harrison's words, 'we give them a future so that they may give us a past'. But, more than this, if the engagement is liturgical – whether the liturgy be over a cup of tea in the home or the reflective awe of an All Souls' service – we enter the sphere in which humanity opens itself both to the mystery of its own nature and to the advent of God's grace. This is not the 'metaphysics of presence' deconstructed by postmodern philosophy, but the Christian liturgical act that Kierkegaard called 'recollection forward' – a reaching out from our home in time to an eschatological 'home' beyond time.

In the inconspicuous, everyday practice of funeral ministry, the priest is carrying out a task that is at the heart of the Church's ministry. Entering the home, he or she speaks of God's love in the reality of here and now. Inviting the newly bereaved into an unfamiliar building which points to another home, he or she speaks of hope in God's love in the mystery of there and then. Participating in the commemoration of the faithful departed, these two spheres of *now* and *not yet* are opened up to one another through the renewing gift of the liturgy. But the Church does not claim to own or control that divine love. For all that the Church has to offer those who seek its ministry at times of bereavement, it also has much to receive. The Church relates to the world *in* God, not *as* God, and humility and patience must be the hallmarks of its ministry. Neither professional nor amateur, through the gift of liturgy the priest can help unfold the sacramentality of creation: the readiness for redemption that characterizes all people at all times and in all places. Funeral ministry is a homecoming to God for priest and bereaved alike. Faithfully and lovingly attended to, it is an opportunity to relearn the truth that the scope of God's activity constantly exceeds the boundaries with which we circumscribe the Church:

'The holiness of the heart's affections.' Never tamper with them. In an age of science everything is analysable but a tear. Everywhere he went, despite his round collar and his licence, he was there to learn rather than teach love. In the simplest of homes there were those who with little schooling and less college had come out top in that sweet examination.

(R. S. Thomas, 'The Echoes Return Slow' in
Collected Later Poems, Bloodaxe, 2004)

*   *   *

Bibliographical Note

The two authors whose influence is nearest to the surface of this chapter are Robert Pogue Harrison and Jean-Yves Lacoste. Harrison's *The Dominion of the Dead* (Chicago University Press, 2003) is a stimulating exploration of the relationship between the living and the dead. Much of Lacoste's work is untranslated, but *Experience and the Absolute: Disputed Questions on the Humanity of Man* (translated by Mark Raftery-Skehan, Fordham University Press, 2004) is a good introduction to the shape of his thought.

Chapter 5

Attention

Jessica Martin

For this chapter the author has offered her own introduction. It reflects the fact that, while carrying out a role, the priest never ceases to be a person. While the struggles of being a person may overwhelm one's own sense of being able to carry out a role, others may yet see the light of Christ shining through what one can oneself only see as cracks. Prayer is central in the constant priestly calling to attention – attention often to the intractable and the unbearable.

> As we have received mercy, we faint not.
> (2 Corinthians 4.1)

This chapter is mundane, rather than parochial: I have no parish. I am a university teacher and a priest, and I live with an intractable family situation which is not so much the chapter's subject as its location. My circumstances are such as to cause me regularly to question my fitness for, though not so far to abandon, my calling. That's a separate thing, maybe. In a sense I am writing about 'private life'. Yet I write as a priest all the same: a curiously invisible and impotent one in a curiously invisible situation (though one which also contrives in some of its aspects to be as public as shame).

To write about prayer at a time when one's ordinary prayer discipline is in tatters is troubling. But the thing which I've called here 'attention' – an apprehension, the presence of God made inexplicably tangible – seems to have arisen out of those tatters. It is prayer, all the same: the prayer of a life at times so beleaguered that it becomes reduced to sharp messages, miniatures, flashes and vanishings. At the centre of it there's an experience of meeting God which – in a sense – solves nothing at all, but which is nevertheless soaked in the unsettling clarity of divine presence. If such moments are elusive (they certainly elude description) they are also everywhere, overflowings from what is, here and now, towards an unimaginable kind of continuously present experience intersecting with and sanctifying our own.

It is at the same time true to say that such moments are rare, short and leave the soul desolate. Or even: the desolation out of which they arise and into which they then fall is somehow the stuff of the encounter. I do not know how.

*   *   *

I walk by the river with the rest of my family. There's a swan on her nest tucked away just below the toy-size vista of Fen Ditton church, the neat green criss-cross of the railway bridge to one side of us, and, running before and behind, the wide sight of coarse grass and seedheads which shift with the wind as if someone were writing on them invisibly. It is Sunday afternoon. Sunday is my daughter's bad day: 'There's no one around.' Drops are slow in town where she busks. She prefers not to spend the day with us because the streets will empty earlier than on weekdays and she needs to raise the amount she needs to use heroin before the shops shut and people go home. We will see her later, for an evening meal, once she's got her money and done her business. Visits of much greater urgency follow the same timetable: a swollen leg, likely to be another deep-vein thrombosis, won't be taken to the hospital until the evening: 'I need something to hold me in case they keep me in.' The nights she eats with us she will thank us for the food with scrupulous courtesy, but she can't always face the eating part. Unwilling to hurt, she'll go to some lengths to hide it, usually under wads of kitchen paper on the side of her plate, and accompanied with assertions of how much she has eaten really, how full she is, how delicious it was. Sometimes she presses on us gifts of food from passers-by, her contribution to the meal. (*Why* do they buy her diet bars, I wonder, when her shoulder-bones stick out like that?)

Her flat is five minutes' walk away from this big sky. Below it, this afternoon, there are young women running and rowing, girls strolling with their families, couples courting, girls walking silky golden dogs. She is as full of beauty, life, vigour and intelligence as any of them; and almost every scrap of the considerable energy and address she possesses is bent to the service of her own slow destruction in a series of identical days for which the most she can hope, and the end towards which she works, is an unanxious sleep – one free of dreams if she is lucky. Opiates send horrifying nightmares. After the supper she could not eat she'll probably make herself a few slices of buttered toast, or a bowl of cereal, washing them down with mugs of sugary tea. She still loves the sorts of things I bought as occasional treats when she was a little girl: chocolate teacakes filled with marshmallow, individual iced cherry bakewells, iced buns, buttered malt loaf. On Tuesday, benefits day, Mr Kipling and his exceedingly good cakes will benefit from her custom along with the day's dealer.

We decide we haven't time to walk all the way over to Fen Ditton, not if we're to get the dinner on for an early evening meal, so we turn back. The air is warm. At the top of the footpath, under a plum tree, a couple of blackbirds regard us with remarkably little fear, the female barely pausing as she tugs at a worm in the grass. An elderly alcoholic woman, a local, sleeps beside them in the shade. There's a hot-air balloon on the horizon. We speed up the little stretch of the journey by swinging the baby up in the air between our hands. Outside the house our big male cat waits for our return with a loyal alert air, rather like a dog. (Any *Beauty and the Beast* bargain with our household would see the Beast conversing in puzzled mews with a fluffy moggy over the napkins and silver.) Otherwise the space outside our house is empty. We hardly ever see my adult child arrive; and when she leaves she seems to vanish faster than even a fast walk quite explains. She's there and not there. Never gone. Never present.

Later. There's no Evensong to do tonight, so I don't have to leave the rest of the family to go to College. We are in that peaceful backwash just before a Sunday meal, full of cooking smells mixed with the sharp scent of a lit rollup coming through the open door. My baby daughter and my grown-up daughter are sitting on the step companionably, considering whether Big Bear, the largest of the teddies, is likely to appear at the window at all: 'Two large furry ears, one shiny wet nose, two big goggly eyes, IT'S A BEAR!' By a happy coincidence Bear tends to visit when my grown-up daughter does. My husband is making gravy and conducting a conversation about Alan Moore and graphic novels fragmented by Bear's exploits and the stealthy but determined attempts of another of the cats to steal the butter. Tonight, so far, is being a good visit, its balance of needs a manageable one.

These small domestic gifts are all we have left to give to a person *in extremis*, and we know they cause her pain as well as some sustenance. Rehab – the last time recent – has not worked. We start the slow process of saving up the money all over again from here. Living with us has not worked. Living without us has not worked. Endless programmes with the local Drug and Alcohol Service have not worked. Methadone certainly has not worked, though it gave her a new addiction to combat and further compromised her already shaky kidney function. The deaths of friends and acquaintances on the street, including an ex-boyfriend, have caused fear and sorrow but not prompted any change of life. Narcotics Anonymous – so far – has not worked. Offers of counselling, therapy and so on, are accepted gratefully but never followed up. It has been like this, with minor variations, for six years.

'I was prayed over again today, on my pitch,' she says, casually. 'They gave me a nice little medallion: look. It's got the Ten Commandments on it.' She brings it out: it certainly is small, perhaps the size of two 50-pence coins placed top to bottom, and the words on it almost illegible. It is made of something like nickel.

'Just as well you have short sight,' I comment. 'Long-sighted buskers must curse a bit.'

'To be honest, though it is nice, I wish it had something different on it. I mean, the *Ten Commandments*. I wish it had a psalm on it, something I could get comfort from. Or strength. Though I did get given a really cool little Bible by someone else. At least they weren't creationists this time.'

'Are they usually?'

'Those Americans who called down the Holy Spirit on me were. They were – very intense, and they – I felt as if I couldn't think straight. They made me feel very faint and ill, and when I said I felt odd they looked very knowing and said that was the Spirit working. Only, well, if it was then not a lot happened apart from feeling like shit for a bit. And frightened. And there's a nice girl, a student, who tells me all about it and gets very surprised when I argue with her about evolution and myths and things. You know, she's doing Natural Sciences! How does she manage that, do you think?'

'I expect', I say, 'that her mind has different sections that don't talk to each other much.'

She gives me a quick look.

'Yes,' she says, 'I expect so.'

A short silence.

'I wanted to tell you about the Americans especially. To know what you thought. I mean, I did feel really strange. I mean, weird things happen, don't they? I felt like something had exploded in my head.'

I hesitate for a long time. In the end I say, cautiously, 'What's your instinct about it?'

'I hated it. I don't think God is like that, not really. It was just, I thought, well, what have I got to lose? Supposing it worked? I wouldn't have to busk up the rest of the money. For a start.'

'I don't think God is a – a kind of magic,' I say, uncomfortably aware of the number of times I ask, continue to ask, for a miracle. 'Not – kazoom, now everything's different. I think. It's been like that for some people, I know. St Paul, sort of. But, even then – I don't think God chooses to override your will, even when it's sort of unfair because other things do.'

She nods. 'I wasn't really agreeing with it. I was holding back. They were so insistent, they – made me want to hold back.'

She pauses.

'Maybe – if I hadn't held back – something would have happened.'

Another pause.

'I know when God comes to see me,' she says. 'I have to ask, always. But I get held. That's the best way I can describe it.'

'Good,' I say, bleakly. 'That's good.'

Next day I cycle to the nursery under a grey sky, settle the baby and leave slowly, daunted by the day ahead. As usual, nursery timings mean that I have missed Morning Prayer in Chapel: it will fall to me to make the time, if I can, resisting the pull of e-mails and undone work. The nursery car park is gravel, this morning full of puddles which have been a fascination to every small child arriving. I stand beside the mature plane tree, one hand against its trunk, steadying myself against the day, and look down. If you stand above a puddle it reflects monochrome but it is not flat. On the contrary, it appears very deep, or possibly very high, and the things it shows you – branches and leaves – hang in the distance. How very extraordinary, I think, to be able to see, to possess but not to reach, this vista of leaves, the soft black corner of a building at the boundary of the reflection. Another self, behind a wooden classroom demolished years ago, gazes into the same pool at the same graphite leaves shining with muted, unapproachable light. *Who going through the vale of misery use it for a well; and the pools are filled with water.*

By evening the night is wet. I am mightily tempted to skip the meeting. The day has been long and difficult, with a distressed and swamped undergraduate wanting to leave (again), a member of staff wanting to talk about an illness at home, a colleague with family troubles. None of these situations, in their individual ways insoluble (two of them chronic, one terminal) have I done more than react to. That's how it feels. They are undigested, unprayed for. There are essays to mark for tomorrow's supervisions. On the other side I am aware that my usual level of distress at our own family situation is high enough to blur and muffle all my other reactions, and the meeting might help with that. It's not long before thinking about, reacting to, attempting to help, your addict overtakes every other activity, trumps every other need around you. So distress is worth keeping an eye on.

Therefore, counter-intuitively, I leave my husband to do the baby's bedtime and get in the car. The dreariness of the wet is sharpened on a Monday, the day before benefits day, by my consciousness that my daughter is probably still out on her pitch in it, and likely to have run out of electricity when she does get home. I put the car in gear and set off, hoping to have pushed the thought away, but it only alters.

In the middle of reading a graduate student's chapter on *Paradise Lost* that day I had suddenly been struck (the word seems scarcely metaphorical) by four sneering lines from Satan about humanity:

> Man
> Plac'd in a Paradise, by our exile
> Made happy: him by fraud I have seduc'd
> From his Creator, and the more to increase
> Your wonder, *with an apple*.

One point of the argument was that Satan only calls the fruit 'an apple' when he has a rhetorical intention to belittle, in two possible ways – either by saying 'It's only an apple, so how can an act of arbitrary disobedience so trivial really mean death?'; or by saying (as here) 'Would you believe those stupid humans giving up Paradise for the sake of *an apple*?' The discussion of the lines was part of a debate about whether the Fall lay in the act of eating itself or whether it lay wholly or partly in the act of will to eat. Elsewhere, Milton uses the word 'fruit' (as at the end of the first line of the whole poem) which collapses together the apple itself and the idea of a consequence, fending off one quite common response to the whole story which is to say how unreasonable God was to make it so vital to be able to resist an apparently unimportant, not to say arbitrary, temptation. I've read a lot of student essays which get quite cross with God about this.

It all sounds kind of trivial – 'academic' – until you've known an addict. As I had read the passage I had remembered the different narrations of successful temptation which were part of our life now. 'You think to yourself, well, I could do with some money for the 'leccy, a tenner would be about right, and you busk up your tenner feeling very virtuous because you're going to put it in the meter, then you think, I've got a tenner in my pocket, I'll just go down *this* street, perhaps I'll go and see so-and-so, then you meet someone who assumes you're there for the reason that – well, for the reason that you *are* there really – and you think, I can't embarrass myself now, I'll go through with it, just because I get something it doesn't mean I have to use it, I'll have it by me just in case, and then it's in your pocket and it's *too late*.' It's hard to see which of any of these preliminary actions could be said to be anything but *in themselves* little and arbitrary, yet they build up to the final one – which is neither – in such a way as to make it almost inevitable. A set of decisions of rather this kind had meant that, only a very few weeks ago, as I drove her back to the rehab she had impulsively left, I drove with her, without knowing it, a bag of heroin. She knew the stakes: on the one hand an uncertain but open future, a chance not only of physical survival but of keeping a foothold in a domestic life she deeply valued; on the other isolation, drudgery, squalor, and monstrously increased chances of dangerous illness or death. Throughout the four-hour journey she chattered like a teenager on her way back to boarding school, or maybe some kind of particularly bizarre summer camp: the people, the art therapy, the music they played on the terrace at nights. She had been pink with health, clean and lively. Last night no amount of make-up could disguise her paleness, the skin covered in acne, the dirt on neck and collarbone, the swollen leg and ankle, blood on her jeans, the fits of blank sleepiness with jaw hanging and hand arrested halfway to her mouth.

And in her pocket, *an apple.*

The day I heard she had left rehab was, by a small mercy, a day set aside for catching up with admin rather than a teaching day. I don't remember what thought process, if any, took me into the town, or how I found myself inside the University Church. My memory of its dimness is also a patchy one; a flash of a distant emotion on entering which might be social embarrassment, in case I looked at all odd or distrait from the outside to the woman selling postcards; a moment of recognition at the flash of gold which was the gilded wooden Lamb of God by the altar. It was quite dark. Votive candles burnt at the entrance to a little side chapel. That seemed something I could do, and I did it. I have another patch of memory, associated with noticing, distantly, rather the way you notice things when vomiting, that the vicar favoured the long thin candles more readily associated with Orthodox worship. The candles lit, there seemed to be nothing left to do, an intolerable thought. Incapable of concentration, I kept feeling as if I were ready for some great but unspecific enterprise of rescue or reversal, but when I turned my attention upon it, it broke up into fragments of a blank exhaustion, as if I had been beyond sleep for several days. This circle of feeling repeated over and over, as it had been doing since the 'phone call, but its repetition within the church building seemed to gain an external, almost visible presence, a kind of turbulence in the air attached somehow to me physically but dancing a little ahead.

I went into the little chapel, 'set aside for private prayer', in flight (I think) from two tourists inspecting an icon, but I neither knelt nor sat. I stood with the whirling sorrow between my hands, and looked up. I have a confused sense of whitewash and pointed spires in what I saw. I did pray. It had words, I think. It may have had a petition, but I don't now remember what it was – which sounds very odd, I know.

I was met. It was not comforting: that is to say, it contained no promises in it beyond itself. Usually my prayers tend to shift uneasily on their petitions, trying to gauge whether there might be any promises in the air into which they are uttered even though I know that my own attempts to control and direct are responsible for the 'signs' I attempt to detect. My struggle with these puerile habits often betrays me into the kind of inattention that cheats me of the presence of God, especially when praying for things I find very urgent. Today I had no bargains to make. I felt that I had nothing left to bargain with – though actually that had always been the case. But for a time, to which I can't give a duration, the whirling air steadied. The picture in my mind is as if a hand and arm stilled the dancing thing and came down to touch my shoulder. It was heavy, though that's not quite right –

uncompromisingly itself. A Person was flatly facing my own grief, and recognizing it. Was facing me. He was giving it back to me, in a way: I felt 'no better'. The future contained exactly the same bleak possibilities. But the Person who faced me knew about grief. And because he knew, I became whole. Neither happier nor better, but for a moment absolutely concentrated within that moment of encounter with someone who held the sorrow between himself and me.

In a manner of speaking the experience did not stop. At the same time it faded quickly, though not as quickly as my desire to draw away from it. It was intense and difficult to contemplate. But its presence holds me together. I know that I managed to weep, and that was a mercy, too. I left the church both single and accompanied.

The drive to the meeting takes me past the Zion Chapel where the Night Shelter is. I look, automatically, at the little group clustered round its door drinking, for people I recognize: Tiger, one-legged now, hunched in his wheelchair, taut, as always, with anger; Flora, whose round features, freckles and long brown hair make her look like a hockey captain but whose history is sadder than that; Jones and Janice and their dogs; Birmingham Sammy, like a red-haired prophet in defeated old age, constantly duped and bullied by the sharper, younger dealers who come down to Cambridge from Tyneside or up from London for the pickings to be had from a naïve and compassionate student population, an affluent city, a liberal welfare and housing policy. Such a small-time businessman – illiterate, himself addicted – introduced my daughter to heroin at more or less the same time as he took over Sammy's long-awaited council accommodation. Sammy is dying now, of complications arising from hepatitis C, but at least when they jailed that lot of Tynesiders he got his house back. No sign of my daughter, but there's a pretty young girl there: probably Emmy, teenage daughter of Jones and Janice, lately discharged from local authority care and until recently making the most of her short reign as pretty princess of the streets. She goes out with young men from the Shelter. She's not on heroin yet, but the last boyfriend died of an overdose after a row, so just now she's never sober. She is 16.

The hall where we meet is painted a glaring yellow. Photographs of, and artwork by, the learning disabled adults who meet here during the day cheer the walls. Nothing in the little kitchen is ever quite clean; the meticulous retired couple who worry about these things have been cleaning and scrubbing for the last 20 minutes. They make me a cup of peppermint tea. We settle round the table, mostly but not exclusively parents, amid a forest of slogans: 'Be kind to yourself'; 'I do not have to accept the unacceptable'; 'It works if you work it'; 'Keep it simple'. Reinhold Niebuhr's prayer is prominent:

> God grant me the serenity to accept the things I cannot
>   change,
> courage to change the things I can
> and the wisdom to know the difference.

Tonight's leader, chosen on a rota basis, reads the official welcome from the laminated card:

'Welcome to the regular Monday night meeting of the Cambridge group of Families Anonymous. Shall we have a moment's silence to remember why we are here?'

The circle tightens around the moment. Nine people breathe together: this unaccustomed mutual focus, neither intense nor unsettling, brightens the air between us. The little group around the Shelter door, my daughter sitting in the doorway of the Alliance and Leicester, other immoveable vistas brought by others here, are recollected into the silence. 'When you come into this room,' (as the leader will shortly say) 'you are no longer alone.' It's an intense relief: the bedrock of the whole enterprise. When I first rang to get details of the meeting, five years ago, the matter-of-fact voice saying 'Oh, yes, my daughter's a heroin addict too' dislodged a burden. Now, each time I sit within the circle, nursing my cup, among this courageous, unremarkable group of men and women, it falls away again, for a while.

We share out the readings which preface every meeting (all the 'Anonymous' groups, whether for sufferers or for their families and friends, are run on a broadly liturgical model pioneered by Alcoholics Anonymous), keeping each laminated sheet face downward according to custom, presumably in order not to be distracted by its contents at the wrong time. The leader continues, eyes down, intent on the card, though all of us by this time could probably manage without it. Reading without much natural expression seems to be another minor custom, as in some branches of the Anglo-Catholic tradition. Or, more likely, people are daunted by long swathes of print. Odd that this group of mostly middle-aged and respectable folk should find it so much trickier, emotionally, to read aloud than the groups of shakily literate men I've seen spiritedly tackling the Narcotics Anonymous readings at prison meetings.

'There is nothing that we as individuals can do to prevent another person's abuse of drugs . . . When we accept drug dependence as an illness . . . we become ready to learn a better way to live.'

We all look up, just a bit, and murmur the ritual courtesy:

'Thank you.'

The readings widen into the group at large, as we share reiterations of the 'Three Destructive Forces' (the first of which is 'the discussion of any religion'), 'Twelve Steps' and 'Twelve Traditions'. In point of fact it has leaked out, indirectly, that quite a number of us will be at church on Sunday in some capacity or other, as well as round this table on a Monday. On Sundays I too will pray for 'the plight of the local homeless and marginalized in our affluent city', and mean it; but today I sit with people who know better than anyone that the only way to keep your beloved from sitting in a public doorway is to buy her, or him, increasingly large quantities of a lethal substance.

It goes against the grain to finance the slow death of one's child – though every person I am sitting with has done it at least once, in a moment of weakness – of pity, or desperation, or under intolerable pressure, or wishing to make the problem go away just for a few hours. When we say so to each other, we find a kind of absolution available nowhere else. From time to time I give – usually women – in doorways money, or food: one terrible Christmas I walked past a desperate weeping girl, she half-drunk and barely conscious of her surroundings, gave her money, certain it was for a bag of heroin, and held her hand, uncertain whether I was doing it because she *wasn't* my child (whom I refused to finance) – or because she might be.

I have been given the last reading: 'Helping'. There's a smothered competitiveness about who might get this, the most popular of all the readings: another reason, perhaps, for the custom of offering them to people face-downwards. I try to read it as if I were hearing it, but it fragments anyway . . . 'not to *do* things for the person I wish to help, but to *be* things' . . . 'I will learn not to mull over the past with regret, or spend time hovering over a future that has yet to arrive' . . . 'I will change contempt for what he does, to respect for the potential within him, and anxiety or over-protectiveness to release with love' . . . 'I will have no thought for the future actions of others, expecting them to be neither worse nor better as time goes on, for in such expectations I am really trying to create. I will love and let be' . . . 'All people are always changing, and I can make that change a positive one, if I am willing' . . . 'I can change myself: others I can only love.' Everyone, no matter how ill at ease with speaking a text, reads the last five words with a simple emphasis which is very touching, as if the loved person were in front of them, but at some formal ceremony where they could only be addressed indirectly.

An attentive pause. Then the ritual response:

'Thank you.'

Today's leader does not fear silence: opening the free part of the meeting (the 'share') she keeps her introductory remarks short and offers no steer for comments. The space left is unembarrassed. When someone's ready, they'll talk about their week, get some misery off their chest, some insecurity narrated to people who know it from the inside; but for now, the silence contains something which puts us where we belong. We are not central to these intractable circumstances, either in guilt or in a potential to save, but properly to one side, listening and being. God, the 'Higher Power' ('which can be' explains a laminated card cautiously 'the power of the group'), is the undefined central space in the order of things we are invited to recognize. It's not just for meetings: 'The intentional turning of the mind towards God', explains one piece of Families Anonymous literature '. . . has to be carried out daily for its fruits to become real.' Like this God himself, it is mundane, as are its lessons of attention. The place where it starts is at the point of absolute helplessness: 'face to face with my inability to manage or control'. That acceptance, 'powerlessness', is at the heart of everything which follows. The advice which follows is invariably flatly practical.

We are learning a lesson in – not exactly loving without hope, but loving without expectations. You love for the sake of loving because there is nothing else left. You may notice and honour a decision for courage in your child, or a temptation briefly withstood, or a kindness, or a delicacy of perception, but you will not be saying to a fellow parent how marvellously so-and-so is doing at university/in the City/at teacher training/with such-and-such an NGO, or how much you are enjoying making plans for their wedding. Addicts don't have futures. The enormous significance such things claim in parental conversation becomes especially visible when you cannot do it. We grieve for those things, in muted form, at meetings, intending not to. They are harmless vanities we cannot have: in their place is the potential for an agony of unspecific, unassignable – the worse for that – guilt and self-reproach. The catchphrases – 'detachment'; 'release with love'; 'let go and let God' – are not recommendations to become cold, or to evade responsibility, but pointers to a purity in the discipline of love demanded: love which is invested neither in future hope nor in the sentimental or agonized memories of a vanished child (a horrible side-effect of addiction is that memory veers unstably between recalling a golden past and reconstructing the symptoms which grimly presage the present, both at their different times convincing), but which celebrates the person in front of you now: blurred, often darkened, sometimes bleakly witty, too anxious to please whoever she is with, patchily vain, a fine whistle player, fearful, perceptive, like every addict deeply self-involved.

The final readings which close the meeting remind us to keep the confidences entrusted to us. We hold hands and repeat:

> Whom we see here,
> What we say here,
> When we leave here,
> Let it stay here.

So I put away, with the leaflets in the box, and the clean coffee cups in the cupboard, some unhappy stories before finding my coat. I look for a while at the tunnel vision of work and busyness which defines my own life, and am disconcerted by the family resemblances between my habits of living and the habits of addiction. If addicts, at least initially, seek extreme short-cuts to an easy mind and a lively spirit, in order to avoid anxiety or sorrow or pain, seduced by myths about 'personal freedom', then what follows is a kind of falling into habits by accident and finding they are – stuck. Gloriously stuck, appallingly stuck; time can't really be passing when nothing changes; the pattern of it (there is no more demanding or monotonous routine) holds them from day to day to day. If they are wearied by age they can make sure they do not notice. A very few years will condemn them unheard. And if the wounded spirit falls into an agony, they have – at least for a time, and at least some of the time – ways to shut it up.

Which is one version of the mundane, of 'ordinary life'. I see, speeded up and exaggerated, my own, ordinary, supposedly unaddicted habits looking back at me: self-deception; unwillingness to face difficulties; readiness to condemn as a defence against shame; short-sightedness; fearful preference for symptomatic relief over healing. And while it's easy for the practising addict to justify using drugs today by fantasizing the marvellous drug-free future, it's extremely difficult to stay clean today in order to have a new and unexpected tomorrow. There are at least two forms of 'living in the present', and at least one of them is malevolent. And I have my own version of that too, where today is to be endured, silence avoided, tomorrow dreaded, daily maintenance always preferred over anything which might bring about unforeseeable changes. To see and believe *now*, to pay attention, seems to take a different discipline from the techniques for shying away from the truths of passing time.

I emerge into a clear, damp evening. Dog roses and lavender brush the side of my skirt on the way to the car, wet with scent. Nothing dramatic has happened, but the space left by our collective silence is still there, light filtering through cloud cover in a big sky. Held in the large space made somehow between my hands is every intractable situation I have encountered that day, and will encounter (the same ones, and new ones) tomorrow and the next day. I am not being required to solve anything, or to perform great feats of faith or marathons of nagging the divine with this or that trouble. But, just for today, I have been given the strength to hold them all towards the unsettling compassion of the Person I let myself encounter from time to time, who stands waiting in the silences, still knowing griefs, still carrying sorrows, stilling tempests, sanctifying the moment.

Chapter 6

Honesty

Andrew Shanks

Coming from Old Byland, as the lane emerges from the over-arching trees, there is Ryedale quietly spread out below, and, on the far side, the hump of Hawnby Hill. Hawnby village appears: one cluster of houses up at the foot of the hill, another separate cluster down below by the bridge. A split village. So it has been from the mid-eighteenth century. And this is why.

One summer's day, back then, two men – Messrs Cornforth and Hugill – were cutting bracken up beyond the village, at Ladhill Gill. Having had a picnic lunch they settled down for a snooze.

And, behold – as they snoozed, they dreamed, both of them, wild, stirring dreams!

When at length they awoke, and compared notes, both men were filled with a powerful sense of God's having spoken to them, and having called them. But to what?

Later that day they went to consult with their neighbour, Mr Chapman. A literate man, Mr Chapman had just been reading a newspaper, which spoke of John Wesley's coming to Newcastle upon Tyne to preach. They sensed that this might be the answer. Hawnby to Newcastle is a 60-mile walk. Undaunted, the three men together set off straight away, up the drove road. Of their journey only one thing is recorded. At an inn on the way they tried a new drink, just being introduced into England in those days: a cup of tea, which they are said to have rather enjoyed. They were ready for all kinds of new experience. At Newcastle, when they heard Mr Wesley, they each underwent a fiery conversion. And once they had returned home, they duly organized their families and friends into a new Methodist community, the first in North Yorkshire.

Not everyone, however, was delighted. All the houses in Hawnby were the property of the Arden estate. And the landlord, Mr Tancred, was a staunch Church of England man. A plaque in Hawnby church records his many civic and domestic virtues. He had the Dreamers prosecuted as, in his phrase, 'lewd fellows of the baser sort', peasants with pretensions way above their proper station, taking the most damnable liberties. And he expelled them, and their people, from their homes.

They set up a rough encampment on the only patch of land available, along the river bank. And there, eventually, they built new homes, the little row of houses that remains to this day, opposite the now sadly disused old Methodist Chapel. This is why the village is in two parts: up the hill is Church of England Hawnby, at the bottom of the hill is the community we expelled.

Up there was where the deferential folk lived. Down the road, the Dreamers.

What is the Church of England? Historically, as an institution, it has all too often been the avowed enemy of all dreamers. For seven years I was priest in charge of Hawnby church, the lovely little medieval place which the Hawnby Dreamers felt compelled to leave – because what went on there had become so spiritless, dull and servile. And I tried to establish a Hawnby Dreamers Day, to commemorate their story. Thank God, the Church of England has now at last had most of its old privilege wrenched away, out of its white-knuckle grip. But the defence of that privilege was the one thing that used to unite us. And now here we are, dizzyingly obliged to reinvent ourselves, without it.

What shall we become? My own dream is of a Church of England transformed into a community of pioneering honesty. A pioneeringly honest ex-oppressor church. It is so much easier to own one's past as something to boast about. And so much more natural to want to remember a history of having been victimized. But for a community like *ours* to be truly honest about its past – that really is a much more interesting challenge.

Also in the parish of Upper Ryedale is the little church of St Mary, Scawton. To step inside it is to step straight back into the twelfth century. It was built in 1146 for Lord Hugh de Malebisse and his retainers, by the Cistercian monks who later went on to build Byland Abbey. And, since the village has always been too poor to afford any 'improvements', the building remains pretty much as the Cistercians left it.

The Malebisse family lived in Scawton only occasionally. Their house there was, in effect, a hunting lodge. But in 1190 Lord Hugh's grandson Richard had it confiscated from him. It was not lost for long – a few years later King John let him buy it back, cheap. For a little while, though, Lord Richard had been in disgrace.

Richard de Malebisse was one of the chief noblemen in York. Only, he was extravagant. He got into serious debt, borrowed money from Jewish moneylenders, and was, it seems, embarrassed by the difficulty of paying it back. At all events, when in 1190 the mob rose up to murder the Jews, he put himself at the head of the murderers. Following the coronation of King Richard the Lionheart, there were pogroms that year throughout the country. However, the one at York was the worst, not least because this was the one place where the mob had a nobleman to lead it.

After the first wave of killing, those Jews who survived – about 150 of them – were given refuge in the wooden keep of the royal castle, on the mound where the thirteenth-century stone structure of Clifford's Tower now stands. The warden let them in, but then left. When he returned, they panicked and locked him out. So he summoned up the militia. The Jews were besieged.

Richard de Malebisse took charge of the siege. It lasted several days. He ordered the Jews to come down and be baptized. If they did so, he promised, their lives would be spared. Each day a monk set up an altar immediately beneath the ramparts, and celebrated Mass for the mob – until he was hit, and killed, by a well-aimed stone falling from above. Eventually, as they began to starve, the Jews despaired. At the urging of their rabbi, Yom Tob of Joigny, many of them resolved to commit mass suicide rather than renounce their Jewish faith. On 16 March, the feast day of *Shabbat ha-Gadol*, after setting fire to the tower in which they were imprisoned, they presented themselves, each in turn, to the rabbi's knife, and offered up their lives as a human sacrifice.

Not all of them, though. For some, trusting in Lord Richard's evangelistic promise of mercy, did come down out of the burning tower, ready to be baptized. But it was to no avail – the promise turned out to be worthless. Now he gave the order: 'Slit their throats, also.'

This was the crime for which he had his hunting estate, briefly, confiscated.

There used to be a rabbinic ban, a *herem*, on Jews living, or even staying the night, in York. This ban was only recently lifted by the Chief Rabbi, Dr Jacobovits. The gentile English, still flush with the virtue of their resistance to Nazism, are often, I find, quite unaware of their own antisemitic past. Yet the fact is, it was in England that that deadliest of fictions, the 'blood-libel', was invented: the paranoid accusation that Jews kidnapped and murdered Christian children, to use their blood for ritual purposes. The first recorded example of this, anywhere in medieval Europe, actually dates from just two years before the building of Scawton church, 1144, when Jews were blamed for the murder of a child (swiftly elevated to the status of 'Saint' William) in Norwich. And then in 1290, exactly a century after the massacre in York, the Jews in England, all of them, were told that, if they did not convert to Christianity, they would be driven out. It was not until Cromwell's day that Jews were once again allowed to live openly, as Jews, in England.

Is the Christian gospel genuinely a vehicle for God's truth? By far the strongest actual evidence to the contrary is surely the history of Christian Jew-hatred. It is so easy to read the gospel in an antisemitic way, yet it is such a complete nullification of the gospel's real truth-potential.

It is so easy.

The revelatory power of the basic Christian symbol-complex 'resurrection of the crucified' derives, originally, from the prior symbolic power already inherent in the Roman penal institution of crucifixion, as an institution. For crucifixion is not just capital punishment: it is capital punishment rendered as dramatically and ostentatiously cruel as possible, in order to make a poetic statement. It is the attempt to affirm, in the most vivid way possible, a certain set of values, supposed to be absolutely necessary for the effective maintenance of civilization. And so it does not just express a verdict on the particular individual victim concerned. Rather, it is designed to express a verdict on the very nature of human individuality. In this sense, not only Jesus but every crucified victim dies as a symbolic representative of all humanity. Crucifixion says that human individuals, simply as such, are worth nothing – 'Just look!' But the one thing that gives individuals worth is their service to the *imperium*, the System.

Nothing could say this more vividly than crucifixion. And nothing, as a result, could say the opposite more vividly than God's resurrection of a crucified free spirit.

Yet, at the same time, the saving truth here depends upon one's grasping the symbol of crucifixion as a representation of everything corruptly repressive in *one's own* culture. The symbol-complex 'resurrection of the crucified' becomes a saving truth only insofar as it is understood as God's verdict on any refusal of the powerful *in general* to heed conscientious dissent from below; and on any collusion of passive bystanders *in general* with such bully-power. What renders it a saving truth is its poetic power, therefore, to challenge *one's own* participation in, or collusion with, bullying. But the challenge is so easy to evade – by the simple expedient of interpreting the symbol, instead, as a verdict on the case of Jesus *alone*. And then there is no real challenge to my own culture, or to myself. There is only a condemnation of those particular others who are supposed to have been responsible in this one case. Namely: 'the Jews'. It is so easy an evasion. And so complete a reversal of the proper dynamics of the symbolism, inasmuch as it positively vindicates a certain sort of bullying; thereby reinforcing the very principle that is meant to be overthrown.

Here then, I would argue, we have by far the most formidable moral objection to Christian faith: that it has, in fact, so often lapsed into such evasiveness. And it seems to me there can be only one at all convincing answer to the objection. Everything depends upon the Church properly confronting this aspect of its history. Indeed, I would argue that it requires our actually devoting some quite serious *liturgical time* to that confrontation – in a way that, up to now, we never have. There is so much to be prayerfully worked through with regard to our historic relationship with Rabbinic Judaism. I think we need to give it regular dedicated time, in our liturgical calendar.

I once saw the Middle Ages all around me; heard it, and smelt it. When I was 17 I went to Ethiopia for a year, to work as a schoolteacher. This was during the last days of his imperial majesty, Haile Selassie. I was in the crowd one day when the Emperor emerged from St George's Cathedral, in the company of President Numeiry of the Sudan, and drove off back to his palace, waving. A small, stiff figure in splendid uniform, radiating stillness.

I have seen a true artist at work, in the performance of majesty!

And then some years later I was curate at St Martin's church in the inner-city Chapeltown area of Leeds, where many of my neighbours were Rastafarians. The Rastas of course revere Haile Selassie as another Christ. Indeed, the actual term 'Rastafarian' derives from Haile Selassie's name prior to his coronation: Ras (that is, Prince) Tafari. Ethiopian emperors have always claimed to be direct descendants of King Solomon and the Queen of Sheba; so he belonged in the lineage of David, as the Messiah is often supposed to. And his struggle against Mussolini's invasion of Ethiopia in 1935–6 made him a symbol of embattled African freedom.

Having observed Haile Selassie's regime in action, I must say I find it hard to accept the Rasta perception of him. Nevertheless, there is much about the larger Rasta project that I think does deserve to be taken quite seriously.

As a Church of England priest, I was to my Rasta neighbours a functionary of 'Babylon'. 'By the rivers of Babylon we sat down and wept', as it says in Psalm 131.1. Rastafarianism is essentially a renewal of that weeping. So the Rastas identify themselves quite directly with the biblical people of Israel, who remembered having once been slaves in Egypt, and who then were exiled in Babylon. They seek to work through their sense of not being comfortable in the society around them by framing that alienation, precisely, as another experience of exile: in their case, from the biblical 'Ethiopia', or Africa in general. And every representative of the British establishment thus becomes for them a functionary of 'Babylon'. Above all: the police. But also the clergy of the Church of England – I am thinking now of one conversation in particular, on Cowper Street, just down from where I lived. A conversation in which I found myself pressed into the role of reluctant apologist for 'Babylon', and found it, I must confess, heavy going.

These were all young people who had been brought up in mostly quite devout Afro-Caribbean Church of England or Methodist families. They rejected the religion of their parents because they felt that it failed to connect with the great historic memory most importantly shaping who they were. Namely: the heritage of the transatlantic slave trade. And, as worshippers of an Ethiopian emperor, they accused their parents, by contrast, of worshipping a 'white god'.

A white god?

Well yes – in a sense, I had to concede the point. The walls of their parents' homes were typically adorned with kitsch icons and calendars, showing Jesus as a rather anaemic northern European, in fancy dress. And when their parents went to church, it was to a late nineteenth-century building, with stained-glass windows featuring the self-same figure. Unmistakably, in this context: the Christ of British imperialism.

These young people had rejected Christian faith because of its entanglement with traditional church propaganda – and because they were allergic to institutionalized dishonesty. I like that.

At the end of the Gospel of Matthew, the risen Jesus commissions his followers to try and capture the imagination of the world at large. 'Go and make disciples of all nations, baptizing them in the name of the Father and of the Son and of the Holy Spirit, teaching them to observe all that I have commanded you; and lo, I am with you always, to the close of the age' (Matthew 28.19–20).

But let us be honest. While the truth of the gospel undoubtedly does require such a commission, it is also constantly endangered by what it thus requires.

The commission was of course highly controversial in the early Church. Not everyone remembered this as being what Jesus taught; many Jewish Christians saw the gospel, on the contrary, as good news addressed to Jews alone. And yet, how could that be? The underlying logic of the argument for a Christian mission to 'all nations' is surely incontrovertible. For, again, it is intrinsic to the basic Christian symbol-complex 'resurrection of the crucified'. Crucifixion, here, symbolically represents the whole element of violence in Roman rule. The violence of Roman rule, in general, was justified by its apologists as a means of uniting many different nations, and different cultures of every sort, into a single structure of civilized order. God's resurrection of a crucified free spirit has to be understood as a symbolic repudiation of everything that crucifixion, as an institution, stood for. And so it points towards a quest for alternatives, better ways of organizing the interaction between different cultures, without the sort of violence on which Roman rule depended.

The Church, then, *is* that quest. It is an attempt to demonstrate, by way of anticipatory practice, what Christ's resurrection politically demands. As such, its whole calling is to embody an exemplary, peaceful communion between people of every different sort. And, to that end, the more culturally diverse its membership, the better. Indeed, *without* the requirement 'to make disciples of all nations' I do not think the gospel would make any real logical sense at all. The essential confrontation between God's judgement and the judgement-system of imperial Rome, as a whole, would then be dissipated. Instead of representing the clash of two quite opposite approaches to the same basic problem – namely, the problem of cosmopolitan civilization-building in general – the drama of Easter would just be the revelation of one particular procurator's most unfortunate mistake!

And yet, at the same time, this missionary requirement is also what most *endangers* the truth of the gospel.

For the constant temptation is to try and go too fast. The true theological basis for Christian mission is the Church's need for the greatest possible well-sustained inner diversity. However, this is all too often corrupted into a sheer impatient desire for greater numbers – the more the better – which is quite a different matter. Already, it seems, some people in the early Church could sense the danger: the evangelist Mark, in particular. At any rate, that is how I would understand Mark's repeated portrayal of Jesus actually forbidding people from spreading news suggestive of his true identity (Mark 1.23–25, 32–34, 40–44; 3.11–12; 5.21–24, 35–43; 7.31–36; 8.22–26, 27–30). Surely, what is intended in these texts is a warning to subsequent generations. We are being challenged to reconsider how we, in our day, communicate the gospel. To what extent do we, in the end, do justice to its enduring proper elusiveness and mystery?

There is – one might perhaps say – a fundamental distinction to be drawn between true *liturgy*, which does do justice to the element of mystery in the gospel, and its corruption into *propaganda*, which does not. Thus, true Christian liturgy is not just different from propaganda. Ideally – I would suggest – it is nothing other than a systematic discipline of therapy against all forms of propaganda-borne moral disease. Only, in actual practice, it is forever degenerating into mere church propaganda, because propaganda is so much easier, so much more effective, so much more likely to produce measurable 'success'.

The point is this. As I would understand it, true liturgy differs from propaganda in the simple sense that it is essentially a celebration of, and a stimulus to, thoughtfulness – in both senses of that word. That is to say: both in the sense that 'thoughtfulness' signifies a kind and generous engagement with other people, and in the sense that it signifies an open-minded engagement with ideas, a genuine readiness to change one's mind. The distinguishing mark of true liturgy is that it seeks – by poetic means, addressing the widest possible public – to break down the interlocking defences of egoistic self-absorption and fixed prejudice. But propaganda, strictly speaking, has no such ambition. It does not try to encourage thoughtfulness, but only to modify behaviour. And it aims to do so in whatever way it can. If appealing to people's egoism will help, propaganda appeals to people's egoism; if appealing to prejudice will help, it appeals to prejudice. Unlike true liturgy, propaganda is not for the sharing of insights. Far rather, it is for the triggering of reflexes.

In the most general terms, one might briefly itemize the standard repertoire of propaganda (so defined) as follows. It may excite raw terror, or it may excite raw lust. Invoking images of glamour, it may seek to latch on to people's envious feelings of self-hatred – with promises of conditional relief. More flatteringly, it may seek to associate its message with people's spiteful contempt for others. Or, promising revenge, it may prey on one social group's hatred of another.

I guess we need a theory of 'just propaganda', analogous to the theory of the 'just war'. No doubt there are at least some altogether necessary messages that need to be disseminated so quickly and so widely, that propaganda is the only way it can be done. Certain public health messages, for instance, may fall into this category; or messages about ecological responsibility. And then, too, the peacefulness of modern democratic societies perhaps to quite a large extent depends upon the efficacy of party political propaganda, getting enough people to feel involved enough in the electoral process for it to be generally accepted as legitimate. I am less sure about the moral justifiability of commercial advertising turned aggressively propagandistic. But one can hardly imagine a modern economy without it.

What is quite certain, on the other hand, is that propaganda can never be used to promote Christian gospel truth.

I am both an intellectual and a priest – one who believes in theology. This makes me feel like a bit of an outsider in contemporary British intellectual culture as a whole.

It seems to me that Anglican theology may well have a great future. But, if so, then it surely has to be admitted that this is in quite striking contrast to its past. Amongst the original churches of the Reformation, the Church of England is perhaps most distinctive for its relative lack of a clear unifying theological identity. Compare the Lutherans and the Calvinists: these are communities whose whole identity, right from the outset, was defined by their adherence to a particular set of systematic theological texts. And as for the Anabaptists, they may have rather less of a classic literature, but even so their dissident identity also rests upon an absolutely clear-cut theological standpoint. The Church of England is different in that what, above all, used to bind us together was just the glue of royal patronage. It was not a theologian who initiated our break from Rome; it was a king, whose dream for the church was precisely to convert it into the most effective possible propaganda agency for the crown. Of course, Protestant intellectuals then joined in, with ideas borrowed from the Continental Reformers. But the Church of England has never, in the first instance, been a church unified by shared ideas. What traditionally united us was shared privilege. And so too, if you compare us to the Roman Catholics – where is our equivalent to the Neo-Thomist tradition? It was not until the nineteenth century that, for the first time, the Church of England produced a truly outstanding original thinker who can properly be described as a theologian. And what happened? Newman found the intellectual environment he had grown up in so stifling that he was driven to leave.

Now that we have, thank God, so very largely lost our old privileged status, and are therefore compelled to reinvent ourselves, there is an excellent chance that things will change in this regard. Indeed, I think the change is already under way. And yet, secular British intellectual culture has inherited, and accentuated, the old Church of England indifference to theology. Indeed, if ever a secular British politician uses the word 'theological', it seems that the automatic association is always with the silly old caricature of medieval scholastic thinkers debating how many angels might dance on a pinhead. So that when, as occasionally happens, one politician accuses another of engaging in 'theological' debate, this evidently means, 'My opponent is an empty-headed pedant, but I, scorning such quibbles, am a down-to-earth pragmatist.'

God help us!

But what is theology really? The way I see it, true theology is in fact a thoroughly down-to-earth, pragmatic discipline. Only, it is all about the building of a form of solidarity that lies beyond conventional politics – *just because it precludes, as a matter of principle, any use of propaganda.* True theology is a devising of strategy – forms of ritual, community organization, education, artistic expression – for developing the very richest and broadest-based sort of solidarity possible, precisely, without resort to propagandist short-cuts.

But of course not all that commonly calls itself 'theology' counts as *true* theology in this sense. On the contrary, all the most 'successful' churches have used, and continue to use, propaganda; and have more or less twisted their thinking to fit what propaganda-success requires.

What I would call true theology actually begins from a heightened allergic sensibility to such twistedness, finding it almost everywhere.

Of the various possible modes of propaganda in general, it is true that Christian propagandists seldom make much appeal to raw lust. But many have specialized in raw terror: first it was vivid imaginings of hell; and then in the mid-nineteenth century John Nelson Darby, most notably, pioneered the modern propaganda notion of the 'Rapture'. When it comes to the glamourization of 'strong' leaders, the Eastern Orthodox and the Roman Catholics may be more old-fashioned in style, the Protestants more modern, but there is equal propaganda potential either way. Christian propaganda typically distorts the category of 'sin', attempting to manipulate people's pathological self-loathing – while the only form of *corporate* sin it recognizes is that of other groups, or other generations. In effect, it promises self-loathing individuals membership in a community of sweet innocence. And of course it has offered the devout plenty of enemies to hate. No longer embattled against pagans, the Western Church of the later Middle Ages was convulsed by wave after wave of persecutory fury: first, and repeatedly, against Jews; then also against Albigensians and other 'heretics'; likewise, against 'lepers'; then, increasingly from the mid-thirteenth century onwards, against gay people and 'witches'.

Anyone whose sole ambition is to gain as many dedicated church-loyalists as possible, as quickly as possible, would be well advised to adopt whatever such methods are available, in their given social context. But one who wants to promote actual gospel truth must, in my view, utterly avoid them – even in their very mildest forms. For what church propaganda conveys, no matter how orthodox it may be, cannot be the gospel. It can only be a simulacrum of the gospel. And it is, I think, the basic task of Christian theology to differentiate between the genuine article and its simulacrum.

Thus, in no sense at all – I am arguing – is gospel truth something that can be abstracted from its means of communication. That is to say, it is not a form of *correctness*. It does not inhere in a set of doctrinal propositions, considered in abstraction from their conversational context. But it is, quite simply, a quality of conversational integrity. Gospel truth is not a form of truth-as-correctness. Rather, it is a discerning, an affirmation, and a disciplined cultivation, of *truth-as-Honesty*.

I write the word 'Honesty', here, with a capital H in order to distinguish the particular sense of the word I intend. Often, in common parlance, when we speak of 'honesty' we mean sincerity: truly meaning what one says. Or we mean candour: truly saying what one thinks. But by 'Honesty' I mean: truly being open to what other people have to say for themselves, and especially those most different from oneself, both by nature and in life-experience. Which, very clearly, means no manipulation. Manipulators may be quite sincere and candid – they only have to delude themselves, which is easy enough if you have a will to it. But Honesty is different.

True Christian faith is surely just perfect Honesty, articulated in Christian terms.

And true Christian theology, as I would understand it, is nothing other than *the science of the sacralization of Honesty, in a church context.**

If gospel truth were a form of truth-as-correctness, then church propaganda would at least sometimes potentially be legitimate. Whatever the short-cuts taken, they would not in that case detract from the intrinsic truth of the basic message conveyed. But, again, I think that the practice of church propaganda is just what *always* most damages the true credibility of the gospel. If divine revelation is God's strategy for the sacralization of Honesty, then the reduction of the gospel to a propaganda message is in every instance a complete miscarriage of that strategy.

Only – is the problem irremediable? No matter how widespread it may be, I do not think so. There exists a remedy, for the simple reason that the corruption depends upon a mistake, which can be rectified.

---

* I have developed this theme, at a more scholarly level, in two books: *Faith in Honesty: The Essential Nature of Theology* (Ashgate, 2005) and *The Other Calling: Theology, Intellectual Vocation and Truth* (Blackwell, 2006).

It depends on mistaking gospel truth for a form of truth-as-correctness.

In fact, true theology, as I understand it, rests on three things. First: a decisive repudiation of church propaganda, even in its most orthodox forms. Second: a confident recognition that the church's historic addiction to propaganda thinking is remediable. And then, third: a principled refusal ever to withdraw from conversation with other Christians, on that basis.

For good conversation does not only mean no manipulation. It surely also means no opting out, into individualistic innocence. And no ganging up, either – I would insist – with like-minded allies, to expel the enemy within.

The current bickering between the leaders of international Anglicanism has generated much threatening talk of 'impaired communion', much lamentation over the dire prospects of 'broken communion'. People on both sides seem to be itching to excommunicate one another, to be freed from the embarrassment of being seen to keep such bad company, and from the constant aggravation of such irritating debate. Some appear to think that sincerity demands it. Or that candour requires it.

But how is such an attitude ever reconcilable with Honesty?

I do not think it can be. And I therefore declare that, so far as I am concerned, I am now, and will always remain, quite unconditionally and with no exceptions, in full communion with *all* those who have been baptized. Others may choose not to reciprocate; that is their affair. But to me this is a matter of basic theological principle.

Does it mean I am condoning evil? No, it would only mean that if the sharing of Communion necessarily implied some degree of moral approval. But, to my mind, it does not. As regards the key issue at stake in the present disputes tearing world Anglicanism apart, the ethical status of homosexuality, my standpoint is as intransigent as anyone's: I regard self-righteous Christian hostility towards gay people as a quite blasphemous evil. The sooner, and the more completely, it goes the way of those other late medieval horrors, murderous Christian Jew-hatred, the impulse to burn heretics, and panic fear of 'lepers' and 'witches', the better. Only, the point is, I do not think of the ideal church as a community of the correct. My idea of the ideal Church is simply that it is a community aspiring to good, Honest – in that sense, prayerful – conversation. What properly binds us together in the Church is not a set of shared opinions. But it is a shared religious language, plus a shared commitment, come what may, to keep talking with one another, as openly as possible. It is in that sense a unity beyond good and evil. True participation in the Church is surely a discipline of *agapé*; an expression of the overflowing sort of love that includes even the enemy. And how can *agapé* think of putting walls up, to shout over? The resurrection of the crucified represents the founding of a new cosmopolitanism, quite different from that promoted by Roman imperial violence, but no less comprehensive – indeed, infinitely comprehensive, as God's *agapé* is infinite. Every act of excommunication is thus, I think, an implicit shrinking back from the promise of the resurrection. To say this is not to condone evil; the resurrection is not God condoning evil! But, insofar as the Church is called to be a remedy against sin, the primary sin in question is none other, surely, than that of refusing true conversation, and preferring to shout.

It may be objected: what about St Paul's teaching in 1 Corinthians 5? Here Paul, in a particular case, explicitly advocates excommunication. The situation is that a member of the Corinthian church has entered into a sexual relationship with his stepmother; and is perhaps invoking his freedom in Christ to justify so doing. Paul, having broken with those who want to keep Christians subject to the whole Mosaic Law, is all the more anxious therefore to try and prevent the church becoming an antinomian sect. And so he insists that the man must be ostracized, both for the community's sake and for his own, in the hope that the shock of ostracism will bring him to his senses. As Paul puts it, he must be 'delivered to Satan for the destruction of the flesh, that his spirit may be saved in the day of the Lord Jesus' (v. 5).

What can I say? Perhaps it was tactically necessary, in that very earliest phase of the Church's development when everything was still so fluid, to head off the threat of rampant antinomianism by such extreme expedients. But God's truth is like a rocket that has been shedding different stages as it goes. And, at all events, I think that it has always been wrong for the later Church to treat this text as some sort of comprehensive license to expel dissidents. In general, I would argue that we need to understand the New Testament as a force-field constituted by two basic kinds of impulse: on the one hand, the implicit logic of the symbol-complex 'resurrection of the crucified'; on the other hand, the tactical requirements of survival, and growth, within an often hostile world. The Pastoral Epistles, for instance, entirely consist of such tactical accommodation and its attendant anxieties. No doubt the accommodation was necessary. And yet it cannot be allowed to have the same authority as what derives from the other impulse, the element of fresh divine revelation in the New Testament, to which it supplies such a very sharply contrasting background.

Nowadays I am on the staff of Manchester Cathedral. One of this church's main claims to historic fame is that on 28 October 1787 it was the scene of the very first large public meeting of the British campaign to abolish slavery. And, in a sense, this was not just a key moment in the development of that one particular movement. But it helps mark the inauguration of a whole new species of political, or perhaps better 'anti-political', enterprise.

In the May of that year the Committee for the Abolition of the Slave Trade had been founded. Previously there had been various tracts published by opponents of slavery, and individual campaigners had fought legal battles seeking to constrain the practice of the trade. But this was the first proper campaigning *organiza-tion* of its kind. And its chief publicist was a young man of 27, Thomas Clarkson.

Shortly after the establishment of the Committee, Clarkson mounted his horse and set off on a fact-finding tour around the chief British slave-trading ports. First he rode to Bristol. There was no welcome for him there. Then, from Bristol he travelled on to Liverpool. In Liverpool he received anonymous written death threats, and at one point had to run for his life, when nearly cornered by thugs who wanted to throw him into the River Mersey. At length he set off back towards London, and so found himself passing through Manchester.

At that time Manchester was a market town just beginning its evolution into an industrial monster. It was already surrounded by a gathering assembly of dark satanic mills; busy processing cotton from the slave plantations of the Caribbean and the southern United States. Yet, no sooner had Clarkson arrived than he was accosted by a group of prominent citizens who insisted that, the next day being Sunday, he should come and deliver an address on the evils of the slave trade, in the 'old church' as it was known. This was a new challenge for him, and, he tells us in his memoirs, not one he had been expecting at all. Nevertheless, he was a natural orator, and rose to the occasion. Arriving at the church, he was startled to find it packed with a sympathetic crowd, including some 40 or 50 black Africans clustered around the pulpit. His hosts had already prepared a petition, and such was the enthusiasm generated by Clarkson's eloquence that in the end this first Manchester petition was signed by nearly 11,000 people, well over a fifth of the entire population of the town at that time. So the movement was launched.

In response to the Abolitionists, the indignant defenders of slavery appealed to the Bible. They cited, in particular, Ephesians 6.5–8, Colossians 3.22–25, 1 Timothy 6.1–2, Titus 2.9–10;

passages in which Christian slaves, far from being told that their servitude is unjust, are on the contrary urged to be obedient to their masters. And if one fails to distinguish adequately between the two elements in the New Testament, the element of fresh revelation and the element of tactical accommodation, then these texts must be reckoned pretty conclusive. But the Abolitionists also claimed to be acting in Christ's name. And surely with far better reason. For what else does the resurrection of the crucified say about slavery, one of the institutions which the sanction of crucifixion ('the slave's punishment') was first and foremost designed to protect, if not that – like everything else crucifixion is designed to protect – it is an abomination in God's sight?

The Abolitionists already to some extent anticipated the later Rasta identification of African slaves transported over the Atlantic with the people of Israel enslaved in Egypt and yearning for an exodus – this was the main theme of Clarkson's address in Manchester that day. They famously circulated the cameo image of a kneeling African slave in chains, with the caption 'Am not I a man and a brother?' And, for instance, they promoted the memoirs of the ex-slave Olaudah Equiano, as a way of awakening imaginative sympathy for all those others who had shared his experience. Here, in short, was an absolutely direct and unmistakable appeal to Honesty.

The date 28 October 1787 was a key moment in the coming to birth of a whole new species of campaign. My proposal is that we call such campaigns 'public conscience movements'. Each is primarily concerned with a different single issue, yet their common feature is an *exclusive* dedication to moral consciousness-raising. Thus, they do not seek any other sort of more coercive power for themselves. Nor do they have much heavy institutional self-interest to defend, liable to interfere with their appeal to Honesty. By definition, authentic public conscience movements, insofar as they are true to their calling, do not make propaganda (in the strict meaning of that term). Like the original Abolitionist movement, they are essentially campaigns for Honesty, and therefore have no proper interest in using any but the most Honest forms of communication.

Beginning for the most part in the 1960s, there has in fact recently been a great proliferation of such movements; or, at any rate, of movements more or less approximating to this ideal. A whole host of organizations has sprung up to campaign for an Honest openness towards voices that might otherwise remain unheard:

- the voices of prisoners of conscience and other victims of tyranny;
- the voices of those officially designated 'the enemy';
- the voices of the poor and the less well educated;
- the voices of minorities traditionally discriminated against;
- the voices of 'foreigners';
- the voices of the not yet born, endangered by our profligate way of life.

The organizations in question are often ephemeral, lacking the sort of deep roots, and the wide range of participants, such as only well-established religious communities have. There can therefore be no question of their *replacing* churches and other such communities; instead, theirs is an essentially complementary role, in the sacralizing of Honesty.

And yet, it seems to me that what the date 28 October 1787 symbolically helps mark is nothing less than the beginning of a new epoch in the history of divine revelation. For are not the public conscience movements of our day, after all, a great new work of the Holy Spirit? I think that their flowering gives us, in principle, a better chance to grasp the inner truth of the gospel than any other generation, before us, has ever had.

Chapter 7

Debate

Grace Davie

This chapter picks up where the previous chapter left off; that is, with the remaining possibility of the Church of England continuing to fulfil a priestly role in relation to the nation. It is precisely the facts of 'secularization' (in the sense of numerical decline in church membership and attendance) which allow a creative re-thinking of this role: a de-potentiated state church still has the power to broker transformed ecumenical and inter-religious relations in a period of religious uncertainty and turmoil. Thus there are things that the Church of England can and does do on the nation's behalf, and debating publicly issues that remain unresolved in the nation's consciousness is one of those things. This essay is an unsentimental consideration of establishment that ponders exactly the kinds of pastoral and representative ministry explored in the foregoing chapters, but with a profound awareness of historical change and passing circumstance. It presupposes a distinction between the notions of 'nation' and 'state': concentration on the latter involves intricate deliberations over constitutional relationships, expectations and entitlements; whereas awareness of the former plays into the terrain mapped by this book, the realm of imagination, association, embedded wisdom and abiding presence.

The argument I wish to propose can be summarized in a sentence. Rather than continuing the debate about whether or not the Church of England should remained aligned to the state, it is more constructive to grasp the ways in which the historic link between church and state can be used creatively in the twenty-first century. In order to do this, I will focus on the English case, but set this in a broader European context. The comparison with France will be highlighted more than once.

I start by considering the nature of the historic churches in Europe, underlining both their links with political power and their hierarchical structure. The *territorial* nature of their organization emerges as a crucial feature. It then describes the different ways in which these links have unravelled, noting in particular the distinctive situation that has emerged in Britain, and within this in England. The following section frames the material in a different way, in the sense that it considers a whole range of factors that need to be taken into account if we are to understand the place of religion in Europe at the present moment. The crucial point to grasp is that these factors push in different directions.

The core of the argument resides, however, in a more detailed analysis of the Church of England as an exemplar of a 'weak' state church – or more accurately a weak *established* church. The situation is by no means perfect, but I will argue that the current position of the Church of England (a powerless, but nonetheless influential institution) can be used to maximize both tolerance and inclusiveness. This would be much more difficult in France. Interestingly, it is also much more difficult in the Anglican Communion, of which the Church of England is the mother church. Here, provincial autonomy is becoming increasingly difficult to manage in a global communion in which the historic sources of power in the North (tradition, wealth and knowledge) are increasingly in tension with the sheer weight of numbers in the South.

The European past: commonality and difference

Three factors are crucial to an understanding of what has become known as 'Europe'. These are the Judaeo–Christian tradition, Greek rationalism and Roman organization. For nearly two millennia, these factors have combined in different ways to form and re-form our understanding of what it means to be European. This will continue to happen. Certain moments in this history are, however, crucial. One such can be found at the time of the Industrial Revolution, an upheaval that radically dislocated a pattern which had been in place for centuries.

The pattern itself reflects two features of the European past – first, that religious power was aligned with political power; and second, that the dominant mode of organization in both cases was territorial. The local resonance of this pattern is as important as the national. European populations lived in 'parishes' (indeed they still do), which were civil as well as ecclesiastical units of administration. You were born in a parish, whether you liked it or not, and – very often – continued to live there for the rest of your life. The parish, moreover, structured the everyday lives of European people: what happened from Monday to Friday was as important as what happened on Sundays. A second point follows from this: the model fitted admirably within the relative stabilities of pre-modern Europe, a period in which the historic churches were dominant. Their power was considerable, with all the associated risks; such churches had the potential to be both excluding and exclusive and at all levels of society.

A model rooted in territory has advantages and disadvantages. Or to put the same point in a different way, permanence is more helpful in some situations than others. It is particularly unhelpful in times of rapid change. One such occurred as Europe began bit by bit to industrialize, and – as the economic changes gathered pace – to urbanize. Populations moved extraordinarily fast to the cities associated with the new centres of industry that were powering Europe. The timing was different in different places, but a church embedded for centuries in the rural landscape was – almost by definition – unable to move fast enough to the cities where its 'people' were now residing. Even now, in much of Europe, there are too many churches in the wrong places. The fact that many of them are architectural gems does not make their management any easier.

The particular nature of the European Enlightenment exacerbated these changes. Indeed it was part and parcel of them, in the sense that it was the new ways of thinking that emerged in and through the Enlightenment that enabled the technological innovations necessary for economic development. But the Enlightenment was more than this: it offered an entirely new conceptualization of the human person and his or her place in society. In some parts of Europe (most notably in France), this became an anti-religious movement: the *lumières* were seen as more a freedom from belief than a freedom to believe (hence Voltaire's infamous cry: *Écrasez l'infâme*). Enlightenment thinkers, moreover, frequently linked arms with the advocates of political change – a combination that exposed the churches to political as well as institutional attack. The result very quickly became a downward spiral: churches that were rooted in territory and supported the traditional order were harassed from all sides, a shock from which they have never fully recovered.

This process affected all European societies, but in somewhat different ways. At one extreme can be found the French case, in which a strict and ideologically motivated separation of church and state took place in 1905 following decades of acrimonious wrangling. France, however, industrialized relatively late, enabling the traditional model to endure well into the postwar period, at least in rural areas. From an institutional point of view, the collapse in France came late, but was all the more cataclysmic when it happened. Something rather similar is now taking place in Spain some 30 to 40 years later. Elsewhere both process and outcome have been different – longer term and less confrontational. The British case is one such. In Britain, for example, new forms of religious life emerged alongside the historic model at a relatively early stage. Some of these grew as rapidly as the cities of which they were part, albeit for different reasons. Nonconformists, for instance, filled the spaces left by the historic church; the Catholic Church catered for new sources of labour coming in from Ireland. Either way, an incipient market was beginning to develop.

The transformations of a pre-industrial and primarily rural society are nonetheless pivotal; they reveal a critical disjunction in the evolution of religious life in Europe. Too quickly, however, the wrong inference was drawn: that is a *necessary* incompatibility between religion *per se* and modern, primarily urban life. This is simply not the case. Something quite different happened in the United States, for example, where territorial embedding had never taken place and economic growth has stimulated rather than inhibited religious activity, not least in urban areas. Hence an upward rather than a downward spiral: in the United States, nation building, economic development and a freedom *to believe* interacted positively with voluntarist forms of religion, which – unlike their European counterparts – were able to move rapidly and effectively into the growing cities of North America. The same has been true in many parts of the developing world; here some of the largest cities house some of the largest churches, not to mention tens of thousands of smaller ones.

The British case

Bearing these points in mind, this chapter concentrates on the British situation, and, within this, on the Church of England.

Some hints have already been given: in Britain, the process of industrialization took place sooner and more gradually than it did elsewhere, and a greater degree of religious pluralism existed from an earlier stage than in many European societies. Enlightenment thinking was also distinctive: it was markedly less ferocious in its attacks on religion than was the case in France, a point made clear in recent scholarship. Conversely, both the Church of England and its Calvinist equivalent in Scotland were 'parish' churches, organized on a territorial basis. They were, therefore, as unable to move fast into the growing cities of industrial Britain as their European counterparts, and for the same reasons. What emerges in fact is a hybrid case: philosophically, there are evident links between Britain and the United States; institutionally, the ties are with Europe.

If Britain can be seen as a midway point between Europe and America, the nature of the Church of England reinforces this position. Its beginnings are quite rightly described as a 'break from Rome', the moment when England (and its church) turned away from Europe and looked out across the world. Anglicanism, unlike most Christian traditions, has no 'home' in continental Europe. It finds its inspiration elsewhere – in a Communion whose shape reflects the Empire. How could it be otherwise? Anglican ways of thinking, moreover, are distinctive, embodying *particular* advantages and disadvantages – a point that underpins much of the following discussion. What on the one hand enables both theological and pastoral generosity, leads on the other to a persistent, sometimes chronic, inability to make decisions. It is equally clear that growing, and ever more vibrant, churches in the global South are exerting new pressures on the Communion – including a need to make decisions, very difficult ones. In a very real sense Anglicanism has become the victim of its own success.

The European present: the factors to take into account

The religious situation in modern Europe is complex. In order to understand both the opportunities and the limitations of the present context, it is necessary to take several factors into account. They are:

1. The role of the historic churches in shaping European culture.
2. An awareness that these churches still have a place at particular moments in the lives of modern Europeans, even though they are no longer able to discipline the beliefs and behaviour of the great majority of the population.
3. An observable change in the churchgoing constituencies of the continent, which operate increasingly on a model of choice rather than a model of obligation or duty.
4. The arrival in Europe of groups of people from many different parts of the world, with very different religious aspirations from those seen in the host societies.
5. The reactions of Europe's secular élites to the increasing salience of religion in public as well as private life.
6. A growing realization that the patterns of religious life in modern Europe should be considered an 'exceptional case' in global terms – they are not a global prototype.

Not all of these can be considered in detail in this chapter; used selectively, however, they provide a framework for the argument that follows.

One way of grasping the significance of the first three is to realize that there are effectively two religious economies running side by side in much of modern Europe, Britain included. The first is the one delivered by history: that is the parochial system outlined above which embeds the churches of Europe into the physical and cultural landscape. This is Europe's cultural heritage. These churches, moreover, work as a 'public utility': just like their parallels in health or welfare, they are there at the point of need for populations who will sooner or later require their services. The fact that these populations see no need to attend these churches on a regular basis does not mean that they are not appreciated.

In my own work, I have used the expression 'vicarious religion' both to describe and explain this situation. By vicarious, I mean the notion of religion performed by an active minority but on behalf of a much larger number, who (implicitly at least) not only understand, but, quite clearly, approve of what the minority is doing. The first half of the definition is relatively straightforward and reflects the everyday meaning of the term – that is, to do something on behalf of someone else (hence the word 'vicar'). The second half is more controversial and is best explored by means of examples. Religion, it seems, can operate vicariously in a wide variety of ways:

- Churches and church leaders perform ritual on behalf of others (notably the occasional offices) – if these services are denied, this causes offence.
- Church leaders and churchgoers believe on behalf of others and incur criticism if they do not do this properly.
- Church leaders and churchgoers embody moral codes on behalf of others, even when those codes have been abandoned by large sections of the populations that they serve.
- Churches, finally, can offer space for the vicarious debate of unresolved issues in modern societies.

The first three of these are admirably illustrated, often very poignantly, by the other chapters in this volume. The last requires a little more explanation, bearing in mind that it offers an innovative way into a specifically Anglican issue. Could it be that churches offer space for debate regarding particular, and often controversial, topics that are difficult to address elsewhere in society? The current discussion about homosexuality in the Church of England can be seen in this light, an interpretation encouraged by the intense media attention directed at this issue – and not only in Britain. Is this simply an internal debate about senior clergy appointments in which different lobbies within the church are exerting pressure? Or is this one way in which society as a whole comes to terms with profound shifts in the moral climate? If the latter is *not* true, it is hard to understand why so much attention is being paid to the churches in this respect. If it *is* true, our thinking must take this factor into account.

With this in mind, I remain convinced that the notion of 'vicarious religion' is helpful in understanding the current situation in both Europe, and, more precisely, in England. It is not, however, the whole story. It is at this point that the second, somewhat newer, religious economy becomes significant – that which concerns Europe's diminishing, but still significant churchgoers (i.e. those who maintain the tradition on behalf of the people described in the previous paragraphs). Here an observable change is quite clearly taking place, best summarized as a shift from a culture of obligation or duty to a culture of consumption or choice. What was once simply imposed (with all the negative connotations of this word), or inherited (a rather more positive spin), becomes instead a matter of personal choice: 'I go to church (or to another religious organization) because I want to, maybe for a short period or maybe for longer, to fulfil a particular rather than a general need in my life and where I will continue my attachment so long as it provides what I want, but I have no *obligation* either to attend in the first place or to continue if I don't want to.'

As such, this pattern is entirely compatible with vicariousness (this is important): 'The churches need to be there in order that I may attend them if I so choose.' The 'chemistry', however, gradually alters, a shift that is discernible in both practice and belief, not to mention the connections between them. There is, for example, an observable change in the patterns of confirmation in the Church of England. The overall number of confirmations has dropped dramatically in the post-war period, evidence once again of institutional decline. In England, though not yet in the Nordic countries, confirmation has ceased to be a teenage rite of passage, but is rather a relatively rare event undertaken as a matter of personal choice by people of all ages. Indeed, there is a very marked rise in the proportion of adult confirmations among the candidates overall – by no means enough, however, to offset the fall among teenagers. In short, membership in the historic churches is beginning to define itself in different ways, which – in this sense at least – become much more like their non-established counterparts. Voluntarism (a market) is beginning to assert itself, regardless of the constitutional position of the churches.

So much for points 1–3 above. The fourth factor is rather different and concerns the growing number of incomers in almost all European societies. There have been two stages in this process. The first was closely linked to the urgent need for labour in the expanding economies of post-war Europe – notably in Britain, France, Germany and the Netherlands. The second wave of immigration occurred somewhat later (the 1990s). It included, in addition to the places listed above, both the Nordic countries and the countries of Mediterranean Europe (Greece, Italy, Spain and Portugal), bearing in mind that the latter have traditionally been countries of emigration rather than immigration. The crucial point to grasp in both cases is that the motives for coming to Europe, both push and pull, were economic.

What, though, are the implications for the religious life of Europe? The short answer is that they vary from place to place depending on both host society and new arrivals. Britain and France offer an instructive comparison. In Britain, immigration has been much more varied than in France, both in terms of provenance and in terms of faith communities. Britain is also a country where ethnicity and religion criss-cross each other in a bewildering variety of ways (only Sikhs and Jews claim ethno–religious identities). In this respect, the situation in France is quite different: here immigration has been largely from the Maghreb, as a result of which France has by far the largest Muslim community in Europe (between 5 and 6 million) – an almost entirely Arab population. Rightly or wrongly, Arab and Muslim have become interchangeable terms in popular parlance in France.

Beneath these differences lies however a common factor: the growing presence of other faith communities in general, and of the Muslim population in particular, is challenging some deeply held European assumptions. The notion that faith is a private matter and should, therefore, be proscribed from public life – notably from the state and from the education system – is widespread in Europe. Conversely, many of those who are currently arriving in this part of the world have markedly different convictions, and offer – simply by their presence – a challenge to the European way of doing things. As a result, European societies have been obliged to reopen debates about the place of religion in public as well as private life – hence the heated controversies about the wearing of the veil in the school system, about the rights or wrongs of publishing material that one faith community in particular finds offensive, and about the location of 'non-European' religious buildings. There have been moments, moreover, when a lack of mutual comprehension, together with an unwillingness to compromise on many of these issues, have led alarmingly fast to dangerous confrontations, both in Europe and beyond.

Such episodes raise a further point: that is the extent to which the secular élites of Europe use these events in order to articulate alternatives – ideological, constitutional and institutional – to religion. It is important to remember, however, that such élites (just like their religious counterparts) vary markedly from place to place, a point at which we rejoin the emphases of the previous section – notably, an awareness that the *process* of religious change has unfolded differently in different places. What in Britain, and indeed in most of Northern Europe, occurred gradually (starting with a de-clericalization of the churches from within at the time of the Reformation), became in France a delayed and much more ideological clash between a hegemonic, heavily clerical church and a much more militant secular state. Hence what Emile Poulat calls 'la guerre des deux Frances', which dominated French political life well into the twentieth century. The legacies still remain in the form of a self-consciously secular élite, and a lingering suspicion concerning religion of all kinds – the more so when this threatens the public sphere. The fact that these threats are no longer Catholic but Muslim does not alter the underlying reaction. In Britain, something rather different has occurred: *overlapping* élites (both religious and secular) work together to encourage mutual respect between different world faiths, a policy admirably illustrated following the bombings in London in July 2005.

Underlying these differences lies a crucially important tension: the complex relationship between democracy and tolerance. This will be developed at greater length in the following section, in a more detailed treatment of the British case. Before doing so, the sixth and final point listed above must be taken into account. It introduces a rather different idea: namely the growing realization that the patterns of religious life in modern Europe should be considered an 'exceptional case' in global terms. In other words, the relative secularity of Europe is unlikely to be repeated elsewhere, however 'modern' the rest of the world might become. Europe is not, therefore, a global prototype. This statement goes straight to the heart of an urgent and as yet unresolved question: is secularization intrinsic or extrinsic to the modernization process? Or to ask the same question in a different way: is Europe secular because it is modern (or at least more modern than other parts of the world), or is it secular because it is European, and has developed along a distinctive pathway? I am increasingly convinced that the latter is the case, in which case Europeans have somehow to remove from their consciousness the notion that what Europe does today, everybody else will do tomorrow. Everybody else, moreover, includes most of the Anglican Communion.

The Church of England: a 'weak' state church

What – within these parameters – is the role of the Church of England in English society at the start of the twenty-first century? The question will be approached in two ways. The first will develop the notion of two co-existing religious economies; the second will elaborate the tension between democracy and tolerance. Both examples have been chosen to illustrate the opportunities open to an established church in a society that is historically Christian, but becoming increasingly plural, and in which religion is becoming more rather than less salient in public life.

Two religious economies

The starting point for this discussion lies in the recognition that the two religious economies running side by side in modern Europe are sociologically as well as theologically explicable, and that both have a right to exist. It is not sensible to force a choice between them, however tempting this might be. Indeed, looked at carefully, each 'economy' corrects the more obvious faults of the other. A public utility can at times be too accepting; a model of choice runs the risk of excluding not only those who make different choices, but those who are unable, or disinclined, to choose at all. Much more effective, in this situation, are policies that support pastorally those (both priests and laity) who find themselves torn between two very different ways of working, a necessarily difficult situation. Any number of examples comes to mind. The changing patterns of confirmation have already been described, a shift that has taken place relatively easily. Much more vexing is the evident confusion about baptism.

Historically, baptism in the Church of England has been as much a mark of Englishness as of Christian conviction, indeed for many people rather more so. There have been several phases in this history – ranging from obligation (more or less rigorously enforced), through encouragement (all are welcome), to a much more selective process in which only the children of the faithful are allowed the sacrament (at least in some parishes). Baptism, in other words, is changing in nature: it is becoming increasingly a sign of membership in a voluntary community, something which is chosen rather than ascribed. Theologies adapt accordingly.

So much is not surprising: here is a church adjusting to new circumstances. Change, however, is painful and for everyone concerned – the more so when it occurs haphazardly and piecemeal. The consequences can be seen both inside and outside the church. Decisions about baptism, for example, divide parishes (sometimes very bitterly), when priest and people take different views, or when the congregation as a whole is split. Too often, moreover, the confusions of the church are projected on to an unwitting population: the blame is placed on those who ask, not on those who make the decisions. But looked at from the outside, the 'logic' is very difficult to discern. Neighbouring parishes do different things for no apparent reason, leading at best to confusion and at worst to an enduring sense of rejection. Without doubt, irreparable damage has been done, a fact evidenced by an endless stream of letters sent to diocesan bishops on precisely this issue.

How, then, can the debate move forward? One point is clear from the outset: a 'weak' established church cannot enforce baptism, nor can it 'make' recalcitrant parishes conform to one or other model. It can, however, learn to live with the tensions set out in the previous paragraph, recognizing that these derive from two very different models of church life, each of which is expressed in a different understanding of Christian initiation. The debate, moreover, should be set in a broader context. The rite of baptism is but one of the occasional offices. And – so far at least – the Church of England has not placed similar conditions on those who require its services at the time of a death. Indeed it is at this point, if no other, that sizeable sections of the English population (just like their European counterparts) continue to touch base with their churches, which respond accordingly. Of course there have been changes, notably the huge increase in the proportion of funerals that take place in a crematorium rather than the parish church, placing corresponding demands on clergy. But care at the point of need, the essence of a public utility, is still very much intact. It is both expected and given, a situation which is unlikely to change in the foreseeable future. It follows that the two religious economies will endure for the time being. And if lessons can be learnt, one surely must lie in the need to avoid the controversies surrounding baptism in the church's care to the dying and the bereaved – bearing in mind that at this moment in the life cycle, the stakes are higher still.

Just how high is revealed in the extract that follows. It is a first-hand account of ministry by one of the Littlemore group. Quite apart from the poignancy of the whole episode, it fits perfectly into the argument of this chapter. This is the more so in that it moves from a far from conventional funeral – and the associated care of the bereaved – to an equally striking baptism, rather than the other way round.

Awakenings

'We're carrying Kenny in!' ushered the arrival of four young alpha males emerging from a densely packed gathering of bereaved humanity. Creased black trousers, buffed shoes, freshly laundered white shirts, scrubbed flesh and gelled hair. Without another word being uttered, the manner of their appearance convinced the funeral director in an instant of their sincerity and resolve as the official pall-bearers were instructed to stand down.

A slow, faltering pilgrimage wended its way into St Michael's. Pews rapidly filled and standing room was soon exhausted, leaving a substantial residue outside. The community had gathered to honour one of its own and to express its grief. A palpable sense of kinship and solidarity pervaded, drawing into an integrity people of various ages and outlooks who otherwise shared little in common. Family, friends and neighbours, teachers, social workers and those with a professional interest, partners in crime, members of warring factions, prisoners chaperoned by their wardens, uneasy individuals trying to look inconspicuous and remain undetected. Evidently, being present for some was a costly business and not without danger.

Such tensions seemed apt given that Kenny had been far from 'risk-adverse'. Last Saturday, an evening of TWOCing [taking a vehicle without consent] ended with a high-speed pursuit when, 'out of his skull' and pursued by the police, Kenny wrapped a recently purloined BMW around a lamppost, killing himself and injuring another. Not that this interpretation of events was foremost in the minds of those present.

For most, Kenny was a martyr – a passionate car fanatic who, denied the wherewithal to acquire his own set of wheels, died pursuing his cause in somebody else's. This was a conviction that reverberated through the lyrics of the joy-riders' anthem chosen for the service, 'Racing 'cross the desert at a hundred miles an hour'.

Yet by whatever criteria one measured Kenny, there was no concealing the wealth of affection in which he was held. A loyal regard that showed no signs of being diminished by his moral ambivalence or recklessness, but seemed able to accommodate these characteristics, and, through doing so, to invest his life with a dignity and worth that it did not obviously merit. This was never more apparent than at the commendation, when those who carried Kenny into church gathered around his coffin once more, and, gripping the timber shell as if it were his flesh, they shared in the priestly act of entrusting, 'Go forth on your journey . . .'

(Ian Wallis)

It is in narratives such as these that we encounter the story of baptisms and confirmations that the more rigorist party might be inclined to suspect. Such stories, however, capture the moral and spiritual complexity of the baptism question. The wise parish priest should tread carefully – flexibility and discernment are likely to be more important than rigor in these frequently very poignant situations.

One rather more prosaic point concludes this section. It concerns statistics. It is important to recognize that comparisons across time and between countries of the proportion of children baptized are very often misleading, for they do not compare like with like. In England, for example, the figures for baptism have fallen dramatically in the post-war period, a drop which requires careful interpretation. At one level, this is – straightforwardly – an index of secularization. At another, it is the result of the confusions set out above. Parishioners are understandably reluctant to bring their children to an institution which appears to reject them.

Interestingly, in the Lutheran churches of the Nordic countries, no such fall has occurred. Here baptism (and indeed confirmation) figures stay very high indeed, reflecting not only a different understanding of the rite, but an entirely different notion of church membership, absent in the English case. That does not mean that the Nordic countries are either more or less secular than Britain; it does mean, however, that they are differently so. In the Lutheran countries of Northern Europe, the public utility quite clearly remains the dominant model. It is supported by church tax, paid by the population as a whole, unless they 'opt out' – which very few of them do. 'Why not?' becomes a very interesting question. Conversely, in terms of baptism, the situation in France is much more similar to that in England; in both countries the rite of Christian initiation is becoming increasingly a symbol of choice rather than obligation. The fact that this shift is occurring in churches with very different theologies, one Catholic and one Protestant, merits very careful consideration. It is not something that could be predicted from the outset.

Democracy and tolerance: a continuing tension
In other respects, however, France and England (indeed Britain) are very different, a contrast that requires further exploration. The essence of the argument is easily summarized: both constitutionally and institutionally France is undoubtedly a more democratic society than Britain. But Britain is more tolerant than France if by tolerance is meant the acceptance of group as well as individual differences, and the right to display symbols of that group membership in public as well as private life. The following paragraphs pay particular attention to the role of a weak state

church in this process which, once again, is in many respects counter-intuitive.

Let us start with the French case. France is markedly more democratic than Britain on almost all institutional or constitutional measures. Here is a republic, with a secular state, two elected chambers, and no privileged church (in the sense of connections to the state). There is a correspondingly strong stress on the equality of all citizens whatever their ethnic or religious identity. As a result, France follows a strongly assimilationist policy towards incomers, with the express intention of eradicating difference – individuals who arrive in France are welcome to maintain their religious belief and practices, provided these are relegated to the private sphere. They are actively discouraged from developing any kind of group identity. Exactly the same point can be put as follows: any loyalty (religious or otherwise) that comes between the citizen and the state is regarded in negative terms. In France, it follows, *communautarisme* is a pejorative word, implying a less than full commitment to the nation embodied in the French state.

Britain is very different. On a strict measure of democracy, Britain fares less well than France – with no written constitution, a monarchy, a half-reformed and so far unelected House of Lords, and an established church. More positively, Britain has a more developed tradition of accommodating group identities (including religious ones) within the framework of British society, a feature that owes a good deal to the relatively greater degree of religious pluralism that has existed in Britain for centuries rather than decades. Hence a markedly different policy towards newcomers: the goal becomes the accommodation of difference rather than its eradication. Rather more provocative, however, are the conclusions that emerge if you look carefully at who, precisely, in British society is advocating religious as opposed to ethnic toleration. Very frequently it turns out to be those in society who do *not* depend on an electoral mandate: the Royal

Family and significant spokespersons in the present House of Lords (where other faith communities are well represented by appointment, not by election).

They are both, of course, intimately connected to the established church, a significant player in its own right. Here the crucial point lies *precisely* in appreciating the difference between an historically strong state church and its modern, somewhat weaker equivalent. The former almost by definition becomes excluding and exclusive; the latter cannot. It can, however, use its still considerable influence to include rather than exclude, to acknowledge rather than to ignore, and to welcome rather than despise. Even more positive are its capacities to create and to sustain a space within society in which faith is taken seriously – doing so by means of its connections with the state. If these things are done well, it would be hard to argue that an established church has no part to play in an increasingly plural society.

One trigger in the continuing controversies about establishment remains, however, the changing nature of society (the process of secularization) and the growth of religious minorities (pluralization). Given these changes, it is argued, an established church is becoming increasingly anomalous: it is less and less able to speak for the majority and it is, necessarily, hostile to minorities. Both issues draw the arguments of this chapter together. The first, for example, can be addressed in terms of 'vicarious' religion. Implicitly, if not explicitly, the Church can – it seems – both act and speak in the name of significant numbers of people, who would not be pleased if such possibilities (the public utility) were suddenly withdrawn. In terms of the second, it is worth looking carefully at who exactly in British society is advocating what. One point becomes clear very quickly: very seldom do the religious minorities (more especially the other faith communities) demand disestablishment. It is not in their interests to do so. It is, conversely, very common for secular élites to argue the case 'in the name' of other faith communities – which is quite a different thing.

Their demands must be resisted. I would, in fact, go further still – and maintain that the debate about establishment is largely a side issue. Much more important is the recognition that faith communities (i.e. collectivities) of all kinds are and must remain an integral part of a tolerant and progressive society. The primary task, therefore, is to find ways of making this possible. Bearing in mind the difficulties experienced in France, it does not seem that a strictly secular state is likely to provide an immediate answer. Much more creative is a long, hard look at what, precisely, history has delivered to us and then to use what is available as imaginatively as possible. The Church of England – in its current form – has clearly a role to play. At the very least, it can act as an umbrella of faith, ensuring that the debate about religion is both constructive in itself and heard by the powers that be. Increasingly, if not always consistently, this role is recognized, not only by the religious minorities but by significant sections of the political class. Religion is bit by bit regaining its place in the public sphere.

Those, conversely, who continue to question establishment fall into two camps. On the one hand can be found the secular élite for the reasons already described; on the other are significant sections of the evangelical community, currently in the ascendant in the Church of England – a group that advocates, with considerable conviction, the model of choice over and above the public utility. Politics, moreover, creates strange bedfellows. It was precisely these two constituencies that, for very different reasons, resisted the legislation regarding 'the incitement to religious hatred'. The secularists feared anything that curtailed the freedom of speech; the evangelicals were apprehensive lest certain forms of evangelism were interpreted as derogatory to other faiths. The challenge for the established church is to mitigate both extremes and to demand courtesy in a debate which, at times, is necessarily robust.

A note on the Anglican Communion

Holding the ring in the English case has a chance of success. Holding the ring in the Anglican Communion is much more difficult. Doing both at once is almost impossible. There is not space in this chapter to develop the global dimensions of the Anglican debate in any detail, except to appreciate that what has been presented as a 'weak' state church in the European context (with its attendant advantages and disadvantages) becomes in global terms a vibrant, varied and growing community of Christians who – for historical reasons – are linked to the Anglican tradition. It is equally important to grasp that the constituent provinces of the Anglican Communion have experienced entirely different histories, and, consequently, find themselves in very different circumstances: some are in dominant positions and some not; some are wealthy and some not; and some, quite clearly, are exposed to very difficult situations, leading at times to outright persecution.

What unites them, especially in the global South, is the sheer weight of numbers, capable of challenging the tradition, precedent, knowledge and power that resides in the North. This is a new situation which has found a focus in the heated, and very divisive, controversy relating to homosexuality, already a touchy subject even in England (see above). The outcome of these complex and painful encounters is far from clear despite the evident flexibilities of Anglicanism if these are compared with the Catholic Church. One thing, however, is certain. The Church of England can no longer ignore what is happening elsewhere; nor can the churches in the North dominate the agenda. Interestingly, the secular press in Britain is beginning to grasp this point. It is as ready to pay attention to these discussions as its religious equivalents. One reason for this lies in the issue itself: homosexuality attracts attention both inside and outside the churches. Another can be found in a growing, if gradual, awareness of the religious factor in the modern world order and its capacity to influence the global agenda.

The modern world, however, is arriving in Europe in all its fullness, bringing with it innovative forms of Christianity as well as other-faith communities. With this in mind, the situation outlined in this chapter could, in a generation or two, look very different. How much more important does it become, therefore, to create a space in British society in which a serious discussion of religious issues is able to take place in a constructive and forward-looking way. The established church has a vital part to play in this process.

*   *   *

Bibliographical Note

Much of the material in this chapter is drawn from my own work, and from the following in particular: 'Religion in Europe in the 21st Century: The Factors to Take into Account', *Archives européennes de sociologie/European Journal of Sociology/Europaeisches Archiv für Soziologie*, 47/2, 2006, pp. 271–96; 'Vicarious Religion: A Methodological Challenge', in N. Ammerman (ed.), *Everyday Religion: Observing Modern Religious Lives*, Oxford University Press, 2006, pp. 21–36; 'Pluralism, Tolerance and Democracy: Theory and Practice in Europe', in T. Banchoff (ed.), *The New Religious Pluralism and Democracy*, Oxford University Press, 2007, pp. 223–42; and *The Sociology of Religion*, Sage, 2007. Full bibliographic references can be found in the last of these.

Epilogue

Rowan Williams
The Archbishop of Canterbury

1

All societies have maps; they give you messages about where you are, in relation to each other and in relation to the landmarks that are scattered around the territory of social life. Learning how to belong unobtrusively in a society is learning how to pick up these messages and identify these landmarks. And societies become confused and fragmented when they have lost the art of communicating and receiving such messages. The maps may still be there, but people have lost confidence in accessing them and understanding them. They become suspicious that others see more than they do themselves and so are able to manipulate them. And if some aspect of the map is forgotten, if some historically inhabited territory is forgotten, there will be a diffuse but deep awareness of being somehow deprived.

British society at the moment is not doing well in its cartography. There is the uncertainty about landmarks that shows itself in our complex attitude to celebrity; the persisting resentment about class divisions, which reinsert themselves in contexts where we thought they had disappeared; the anxiety over what 'really' constitutes British identity; and much more. Significantly, we are aware of a tension not very easy to articulate around religion: the recognition that, among the historic landmarks of our social life, the monuments of Christendom largely jostle against the insistent reminders that we cannot take for granted any specific religious foundation for national belonging, public morality or policy-making. Language about our 'multicultural' character continues to cause confusion and sometimes anger; and the use of Christian imagery or mythology to reinforce what is seen as a threatened national heritage is a deeply uncomfortable symbol of how tangled various threads have become here (think of the odd phenomenon of the revival of the cross of St George in the past two or three decades as a mark of aggressive Englishness).

And for those in our society who still care about – and even practise – the Christian religion, the confusion is not noticeably less. For some, the whole question of what is meant by the Christian responsibility for the nation is to do with the need for more and more vocal and targeted advocacy for Christian morality in the public sphere, most often in relation to matters around family and sexuality, though also raising a voice about what is perceived as blasphemy. Others are prepared to let the public sphere look after itself, so long as the religious community itself grows and thrives in its own terms. Others again insist on the vital role of the Church as a guardian of social capital in the widest sense, irrespective of its actual numbers or of the measurable difference it makes. Most of us probably exhibit more than one of these responses at various times. But what they all lack – and what the essays in this book have tried to supply – is a coherent account both of what the map of our society really looks like and of where the Church's territory is; and they seek to respond by directing our attention to the theme of priesthood.

So, if we try to draw out a bit further how this works – these discussions take for granted some basic presuppositions about religion in human society. They assume that the Church exists because there really are two dimensions to the reality we inhabit, and there really is a need to understand and cope with the question of how we appropriately and consciously live in both. Or, to put it another way, the Church exists because the relations that define who we are are not confined to what we can see and control in routine ways. This is simply to say that the Church exists for all the reasons that any religious repertoire for speaking and acting exists – but, as we shall see, there is something distinctive about the Church over against other such repertoires. In general religious terms, human beings need to develop the skills to orientate themselves properly in that unseen frame for their lives to which they are in fact already related, whether they know it (or like it) or not. And the articulation of those skills and the responsibility for passing them on in the most effective way have been among the factors creating a priesthood, a body of designated interpreters of the tradition and animators of communal ritual; people whose task it is to inhabit the two levels or registers of reality and move between them so that they don't jar against one another destructively. A human community that loses or blocks out the sense of how to relate appropriately to something that is prior to and greater than its own preoccupations is one that will not know how to limit or control its anxiety, its rivalry and thus, ultimately, its violence.

2

But Christianity has, from the first, had complex ideas about priesthood. Priesthood works, classically, through the supervision of *sacrifice*, the processes by which peacemaking gifts are offered to the divine so that sacred order may be restored, so that the two registers of reality 'fit together' again after the various sorts of rupture that make them jar. The Christian narrative announces that there is one moment in human history that so unites the different realities in relation to which human beings live that there is never again going to be a need for any 'priestly' mediation between them; all future crises of disjunction are foreseen and included in this event, and resolved with reference to it.

Priesthood is over and sacrifice is now unnecessary. That is what the Christian gospel says, at first sight: Jesus has offered his life 'once, only once, and once for all', and the distinctive anxieties of religion are behind us for ever. More specifically, this is what the Reformation reaffirmed, with some violence, in the belief that the Church had in effect reinstated a system of priesthood where none was needed, thus compromising the uniqueness of the action and suffering of Jesus in his crucifixion.

But in fact this represents a damagingly limited reading of the gospel. It is not that the categories of priesthood and sacrifice have been evacuated of meaning: they have been drastically re-imagined. It is true that the action of Christ on the cross becomes the pivot of the whole of human history and so defines, once and for all, what priesthood is. Heaven and earth are reconciled not by an anxious negotiation over what might count as an adequate propitiatory gift but by an act of self-displacement in which the ultimate source of sacred power declares itself free to restore any and every breakage of relationship, irrespective of what human beings try to do to mend things. 'Priesthood' as exercised by Jesus incarnate and crucified is about the history of a life that moves towards one focal moment in which the divine relinquishes claims against humanity and the human accepts the full consequence of divine presence in a violent world. It is about the coincidence of two acts of self-displacement performed in and by one agent, divine and human at once.

To try and spell this out a bit: in the crucifixion of Jesus, God, by accepting the defeat of extreme dereliction and mortality, defines his love for the world as one that cannot enforce any claim, cannot triumphantly resist or overcome any rejection. The God who is seen on the cross is one who refuses to defend his 'territory'. And he is present in this supremely paradoxical way in

and through a human life that likewise refuses to defend its territory, a life in which God is free to pervade every moment, thought
and action – a life surrendered to God. The cross is what happens
when there are no barriers between God and humanity; when
what has been called the 'kenosis', the self-emptying, of both is at
its most unreserved.

The effect of this, says the New Testament, is to create a
pathway or an open door between earth and heaven that no turn
of events in the world can ever again close. A place has been
cleared where the act of God and human reality are allowed to
belong together without rivalry or fear: the place where Jesus is. It
is a place where human beings have only to be open to what is
offered and where God demands nothing and imposes nothing
but simply abides in unceasing love, a love that can only be
imagined in the human world and human language in terms of
vulnerability. It is thus a place where human competition means
nothing; a place where the desperate anxiety to please God means
nothing; a place where the admission of failure is not the end but
the beginning; a place from which no one is excluded in advance.

What has opened this place or doorway – variously imagined
in the New Testament as a place in which to live and as a journey
to travel – is the action of Jesus; and as something that reconnects
alienated worlds, the sacred and the fallen, damaged or compromised, it can be spoken of as priestly, and as priestly in a way that
no other action can ever again be priestly, since it marks the end
of all anxiety about how reconciliation is to be achieved. In the
sense that no person will ever now be a priest in the sense Jesus is,
it is true that priesthood is over. But – and it is a massive qualifi-
cation, regularly overlooked or misunderstood – what the New
Testament plainly says is that the effect of this priestly action is
to bring the community united with Jesus into the place he
occupies, so that they can be called 'priestly' (1 Peter 2.9 and
Revelation 22.4 are two of the most unambiguous texts on this).

The role of the community in the world is to inhabit the place where Jesus' priesthood has been exercised; their style of life, action and prayer becomes the channel by which priestliness is made real and accessible in the world. The Church, then, as the historical Body of the one High Priest, occupies the place where competition and anxiety and violence are exposed as meaningless, as the acting out of destructive and compulsive fantasies; the place where it is possible to fail, to need, and to let down defences.

3

Thinking about religion in general (never actually a very sensible idea, but it has to be done sometimes) brings us up against the apparent unavoidability of a place on the social map where people are reconnected with the sense of a prior and larger order of reality, a reconnection that regularly appears as involving cost (sacrifice). But the proclamation of the Christian good news tells us that this place on the map doesn't have to be constantly reinvented or cleared afresh: it is a secure place, both in the sense that it is indestructible and in the sense that it is safe for the most vulnerable. The task of priesthood, the task of mediating between orders of reality, is now something that has to be witnessed to rather than performed anew or independently; and it is a task committed to those who have come to be at home in the place marked out by Jesus. For human beings, priestliness is now bound up with faithfully occupying the area where divine and human action decisively overlap in Jesus and making sure that the human world knows that there is such a place.

So where the priestly people are to be found is where there is a certain kind of space for human beings, a space that does not belong to any sub-section of the human race, but – because it is first the space cleared by God – is understood as a space where humanity as such is welcome. It is not defended against anyone;

it exists because of the defencelessness of God in the crucified Jesus. Those who occupy it are not charged with marking it out as a territory sharply defined over against territory that is the property of others; they are to sustain it as a welcoming place. This is not to say that it is simply a neutral spot where nothing happens; on the contrary, those who enter this space expose themselves, knowingly or not, to a radical readjustment of their relations to their familiar reality because they are being introduced into a new relation with the sacred, with the love of God. In that sense, it can be an unsettling, even a frightening place in which to be, where love and what the New Testament calls 'wrath' may often be indistinguishable – where there is a burning abrasion between old habits and the new reality. But it is not the job of the priestly people to 'administer' this, only to hold the door open.

The Church as a human community and the actual physical places where it is regularly encountered (usually but not exclusively church buildings) provide the room for those aspects of human experience that will not fit anywhere else – a formulation I owe to a former student, Gillean Craig. The dimensions of humanity that are disadvantaged or ignored in the world where what matters is managing relations that are always potentially threatening and patrolling territories that are always threatened – these are the dimensions that are accommodated in the life of the Church, in the territory that is not defended or patrolled but claims to be potentially everyone's. And for the Church to make this credible and effective requires of the Church a rigorous collective self-displacement, a readiness constantly to question itself as to how far it has yielded to the temptation of territorial anxiety. Not that it is a community or a set of practices that have no coherence and limits; more that those limits are there to conserve the radical character of the welcome offered; because without the central commitment to the inseparable divine and human action that clears the space, none of this would really make sense. But the only kind of anxiety that is proper to the

Church is what prompts careful self-scrutiny as to whether we have begun to take for granted the map offered by the contemporary world, a map in which there is finally no place free from rivalry and thus potential violence.

All this is a laboured attempt to 'locate' what the essays in this book have been about. Some describe what it is like to find yourself, not by any conscious decision but because this is how the world works, carrying the otherwise unbearable grief and shock of a community living with trauma – with a child's murder, to take the most challenging example – where there is no other body that can meaningfully accompany a community's suffering, and indeed the suffering of certain individuals within it. Others speak, directly or indirectly, about the Church as the only community that has the experience and authority to offer to its surrounding culture words for repentance, words for a shared grief over a past that can never be anything other than a record of failure or betrayal, yet which is somehow located afresh by being named honestly for what it is by people who are not ashamed of naming failure. Others chart the way in which belonging in the Church is and is not like other sorts of radically celebratory ways of human sharing. All assume that the mixed and not always edifying history of the Church of England's relations with the national culture in which it is set curiously draws out in its pastoral ministry something crucial about the gospel: it outlines a territory that is in some respects coterminous with the limits of the community itself and yet which cannot now be seen in the ways it once enjoyed and sanctioned, as a guarantee of unifying ideological loyalty. The most paradoxical but most insightful accounts of the Church of England in this book are those which suggest that a church occupying the shell of national political significance but having lost much of the substance is peculiarly well placed to communicate something of the central vision of an undefended territory created by

God's displacement of divine power from heaven to earth and the cross.

And what these essays also and so very importantly affirm is that this priestliness in respect of the society we inhabit is focused in the persons of the Church of England's priests. From the Church's point of view, the ordained ministry exists to remind the Church what it is, to tell it daily by the recital of the word and the performance of the sacraments that it does not exist by its own resolution and does not define its place for itself and by itself. The ordained ministry is there to speak of the Church's transcendent origin and horizon, to witness to the nature of the space that God clears. It is necessary to the Church because of our innate drawing towards what I earlier called territorial anxiety; it is the servant of the Church's honesty (its repentance, its gratitude). But this means that from the point of view of the society around, the ordained minister, the person who embodies the particular kind of priestliness that is the heart of the Church's calling, shares in the public perception the same important unclarity that hangs around the Church of England's identity: the same vulnerability to dismissive or derisive perception on the one hand, the same vulnerability to endless and shapeless demands on the other.

Priesthood in the Church of England as exhibited here is crucially to do with the service of the space cleared by God; with the holding open of a door into a place where a damaged and confused humanity is able to move slowly into the room made available, and understand that it is accompanied and heard in all its variety and unmanageability and emotional turmoil and spiritual uncertainty. And as at least one of these essays also spells out in harrowing detail, it is a priesthood that may be nourished on the soil of your own emotional turmoil and spiritual uncertainty; the faithful carrying of the traumas of a community is not something that can be learned without some degree of faithfulness and patience in the place where you yourself learn that there is room for the unmanageable grief of a love that feels helpless and defeated.

But in case anyone might suspect that the heart of priesthood was simply an emotional wasteland in which the ordained priest did nothing but carry the load that society can't bear, we are also reminded here of the one irreplaceable action that makes the priest what she or he is: the animation of the believing community's thanksgiving, its corporate acknowledgement of where it has been brought, its appropriation for itself in constantly changing circumstances of the fact that a place has been opened for humanity where Jesus stands. What priests do is to secure the opportunity for the priestly people to announce who they are – to themselves, but also to the world around; they are trustees of the time and space for worship that can be characterized as the action of the whole of the believing community, not just of a group of individuals, whether large or small. We are so used to rejecting indignantly the idea that all clergy do is 'take services' that we are in some danger of forgetting that if they don't do this they are not doing what they are asked to do. For them to be servants of the space cleared by God, they must be at the service of the community's need to express its common gratitude in a shared language, in a time that is given up to this and nothing else. The traditional Anglican and Catholic obligation to say the 'daily offices', Morning and Evening Prayer, is the tangible sign of the obligation to see to it that the community's worship happens – and happens in such a way and such a style that it declares plainly something of the nature of the place Christians believe they occupy. To be a liturgist – a person whose skills are directed towards making or letting the corporate action of the community at worship happen with integrity and depth – is not an optional extra for the priest. The priest keeps open the space human society needs by taking the responsibility for inviting the believing community back again and again into this space, so that the society around can see that it is still, indestructibly and non-negotiably, there.

4

Being a priest is not first about 'leadership' – though that is not an irrelevant concept if it is properly understood as identifying the differences that can and need to be made in a community, and seeing that they happen. It is not primarily about the role of organizing and administering, but neither is it in any simple sense just the role of what one Christian tradition calls a 'teaching elder'. The teaching, like the leadership, happens only as and when the priest has learned what it is to inhabit a place and to speak from that place into the community's life – the believing community but also the wider human community. The lifelong commitment that has been regarded as a necessary aspect of priestliness in the Catholic and most of the mainstream Protestant tradition is to do with this awareness of being called first of all to live somewhere and to become a native of this place. This book has been about how the Christian gospel claims its location on the map of human societies – not by setting up a distinctive territory that has to be defended by any means possible against others, but by announcing that there is space for humanity to be itself and to receive what it needs to grow and be healed, a place where God's initiative in Jesus' life and death and resurrection has decisively made room for the human creation so that there is no more anxiety, no more negotiating, no more struggling to find the currency for mediation between earth and heaven. The fragile and often confused exercise of the pastoral ministry in an established church with an ambiguous history shows itself to be unexpectedly well equipped to witness to this insight about the place of Jesus as every place in the human world and no place in the human world: every place because there is no territory firmly marked in rivalry with others, no place because it cannot be mapped onto any plan that we can conceive. The priest remains the celebrant of what will not fit anywhere else, in the name of a divine act that refuses all self-justification, all successful ways of managing the relation between divine and human. That relation has been taken up once and for all into the inseparable oneness of gift and sacrifice in Jesus. And the priestly ministries narrated and reflected on here proclaim just why and how this is good news for faithful and non-faithful or unfaithful alike.

+ *Rowan Cantuar:*
Lambeth Palace, Christmas 2007

Four Poems

David Scott

A Priest at the Door

I sit at the door of the church
and see who comes in and who goes out.
They don't hand anything in
like they used to, animals or grain.
I don't have to receive anything
to put on the altar, or pass anything
to my assistant to be slaughtered
and the blood drained and flung.
I am grateful for that, not
having been brought up to it.
Instead they get books and papers
snippets of news, and the magazine.
Somebody else does all that.
I have no ephod to divine the truth,
no incense to burn, no curtain,
to close behind me. I have only the agony
of knowing I have little,
and the slow job of resisting
any attempt to make it more, because
in my mind's eye I have the eye of the needle,
and how easy it is for even
licked thread to miss getting through.

Parish Visit

Going about something quite different,
begging quiet entrance
with nothing in my bag, I land
on the other side of the red painted step
hoping things will take effect.
The space in the house is ten months old
and time has not yet filled it up,
nor is the headstone carved.
He died when he was twenty
and she was practised at drawing
him back from the brink
cajoling in spoons of soup.
We make little runs at understanding
as the winter afternoon
lights up the clothes on the rack;
we make so many
the glow in the grate almost
dips below the horizon,
but does not quite go out.
It is a timely hint
and I make for the door and the dark yard,
warmed by the tea,
talking about things quite different.

A Nun on the Platform

She seems in place here,
as much as in the convent,
self-contained, neat
You could hardly call it luggage.

No frantic balancing of cups,
but like a swan, which also
has no hands for magazines,
she stands complete.

No intermediate, half unsureness
no drawing kids back from the edge,
or disappointment over missing,
or expectation of arrival

of a train, leans her,
like the rest of us, out of true.
We are all some distance from our roots
on this platform, but she seems at home,

as her Sisters will be
in the over large garden
reaching for tall fruits,
their thoughts ripening for pardon.

Seeing a nun on a platform
gives the day a jolt,
like an act of kindness,
or a pain that halts.

(All from *Collected Poems*, Bloodaxe, 1998)

This Meadow, a Soul

Left to grow beautiful
the grassy heads do gentle talking,
and as a whole move to an unseen hand,
this way and that. The size of a soul
is like this, just let to be, to breathe,
to bathe in its own space. God has every
confidence in it, resisting continual visits
to check how it's going. It's going all right.
Occasionally a secret breath unseen
blows joy across its face
and in return the soul picks up its skirts
and makes long swathes in meadow lengths of space.

(From *Piecing Together*, Bloodaxe, 2005)

A Note on the Littlemore Conference

Samuel Wells

The imagination of the nation

At his inaugural press conference as Archbishop of Canterbury, Rowan Williams spoke of recapturing the imagination of the nation. Among those who were inspired by this vision were Sarah Coakley and me. Sarah has a unique gift for gathering together diverse people around common themes in an atmosphere of profound spiritual engagement and significant academic rigour. In my own work, imagination has played an important role. I have been among those who have advocated that the study of Christian ethics focus less upon the dilemmas of decision-making than on the formation of character. The formation of character is a matter of shaping what one takes for granted – and thus of nurturing a truly theological imagination that beats with the rhythm of God's drum.

When we first met to envisage the Littlemore Conference, Sarah was a full-time academic theologian at Harvard with a grounding in two parish contexts, one in Waban, Massachusetts and the other in Littlemore, Oxford. I was a parish priest in Cambridge, England, with a sustained interest in writing theology on both an academic and more popular level. Sarah's experience with the social deprivation and dislocation of Littlemore res- onated with the ten years I had previously spent living and serving in socially marginalized areas. And we were both struck by Rowan Williams' observation in his installation sermon in Canterbury Cathedral that if one was going through a time of dryness or wilderness in one's sense of God, the best thing to do was to go and find others who were experiencing discovery by God and renewal – and, likely as not, such people would be found in some of the most economically challenging neighbourhoods of the land. This crystallized the threefold character of the Littlemore enterprise: a rootedness in parish ministry, notably in the context of poverty; an interest in academic theology, particularly among younger and emerging clergy; and a sense that there was something that could be called 'the imagination of the nation' that was worth trying to gauge and inspire.

The imagination of the parish

A mixture of personal experience, anecdotal evidence and intuitive conviction led us to believe that there is a neglected wisdom in the Church that needs to be tapped and celebrated: this lies in parishes where a cleric with advanced theological training has nonetheless chosen to lead a dedicated (and often difficult or ostensibly unrewarding) life devoted to the cure of souls. This vocation is itself of course an English tradition of great distinction; but today – in a paradoxical situation where Anglican academic theology is undergoing extraordinary revival, but numbers of Anglican worshippers are simultaneously sinking dramatically – we believe it requires new celebration.

Thus in consultation with a large number of diocesan bishops, Sarah and I put together a group of such clergy – mostly younger, from across the spectrum of liturgical and theological niches, some established authors and others established parish priests. We enriched the conversation with representatives from other Christian denominations, to ensure this was not a narrowly or smugly Anglican enquiry; with those who could speak to socio-logical and inter-faith dimensions of imagination and society, to set the discussion within the realities of contemporary history; with those who could identify with faithful conceptions of dis-cipleship and social change that went beyond the parish system; with those who were grounded in the life of prayer and the disci-plines of monastic community; and with more than one poet and musician. And we chose to meet in Littlemore itself, in a parish context, surrounded by the mundanity and glory of an English church and parish, by the complex and potentially hostile environment of social deprivation, and within the confines of John Henry Newman's own tiny historic college, with its reso-nances of prayer, theological study and imagination. The College is now inhabited by the Roman Catholic Sisters of the Family of *das Werk*: without their remarkable ecumenical hospitality and support, the conference could not have been what it was.

The imagination of the meeting

Most of the participants, including Sarah and I, experienced the conference, held over four days in the hot summer of August 2005, as the tide turned in the Ashes series and global warming seemed to be taking place before our eyes, among the most pro-found interplays of prayer, creativity, theological reflection and exchange of parochial wisdom that we had known.

What made it so? First, there was the presence of Archbishop Rowan himself, a person who embodies the difficult tension between the poetry of prayer and theological insight, and the prose of overseeing the life of Anglicanism at home and abroad. Second, it was the way the consultations were enveloped in the rhythm of the office (both in the parish church and at the College), the daily Eucharist, and sustained periods of corporate silent prayer, guided by the parish priest Bernhard Schünemann, and enriched by the ministry of the Revd Margreet Armitstead. Third, the imagination of the group was tesellated by various artistic interludes: a string quartet (in which both Bernhard Schünemann and Sr Judith SLG took part); the first performance by Christopher Watson (tenor) and Edith Coakley (viola) of a specially commissioned new setting of 'Lead, kindly light' by Michael Martin; the singing by a group of four excellent young musicians at the Eucharist; and a memorable poetry recital by David Scott and Rowan Williams in the nave of the church. Fourth, the conversation continued over meals provided with great kindness by the people of Littlemore. And fifth, the participants, from their careful preparation of materials before the conference to their cherishing of one another's contributions during the conference, made the whole event a prayer.

One other dimension that most were unaware of at the time of the meeting was that more than half of the clerical participants were to move posts shortly after the conference. There was perhaps a wistful, reflective mood of some things coming to an end, and a deep desire to glean from such experiences all the good harvest that God had fostered there.

The participants included Michael Barnes SJ, Geoffrey Burn, Stephen Cherry, Sarah Coakley, Grace Davie, Mike Gilbertson, Sr Judith SLG, Jessica Martin, Edmund Newey, Hannah Reed, David Scott, Steven Shakespeare, Andrew Shanks, Ian Wallis, Frankie Ward, Sam Wells, Peter Wilcox and Rowan Williams.

The conference could not have gone forward without the financial generosity of Lambeth Palace, two Anglican religious communities, several English dioceses, and a number of kind individual donors in England and the United States. We are greatly indebted to them.

The Littlemore Group, now with slightly changed membership, continues to meet and reflect theologically.

List of Contributors

The Revd Canon Dr Stephen Cherry
Stephen Cherry is Director of Ministry of the Diocese of Durham and a Canon Residentiary of Durham Cathedral. He was Rector of All Saints with Holy Trinity Loughborough from 1994 to 2006, and, before that, Chaplain of King's College, Cambridge. His PhD was on the theology of forgiveness and he contributed a chapter on the South African TRC to Watts and Gulliford, *Forgiveness in Context*, T & T Clark, 2004.

The Revd Professor Sarah Coakley
Sarah Coakley is Norris-Hulse Professor of Divinity at Cambridge University. She previously taught at Lancaster, Oxford and Harvard Universities, and was ordained as a non-stipendiary minister in the Diocese of Oxford in 2000. From 2000 to 2008 she served as an assistant curate at Littlemore during the summer months, and in the parish of the Good Shepherd, Waban, Massachusetts during the academic year. She has written a number of books on systematic theology, philosophy of religion, and spirituality, including *Powers and Submissions* (Blackwell, 2002), and *God, Sexuality and the Self* (CUP, forthcoming).

Professor Grace Davie
Grace Davie has a personal chair in the Sociology of Religion in the University of Exeter. In addition to numerous chapters and articles,

she is the author of *Religion in Britain Since 1945* (Blackwell, 1994), *Religion in Modern Europe: A Memory Mutates* (Oxford University Press, 2000), *Europe: The Exceptional Case* (Darton, Longman & Todd, 2002) and *The Sociology of Religion* (Sage, 2007). She is a Lay Canon of the Diocese of Europe and served on the Doctrine Commission that produced *Being Human: A Christian Understanding of Personhood* in 2003.

The Revd Dr Jessica Martin

Jessica Martin is College Lecturer in English Literature and Fellow in Holy Orders at Trinity College, Cambridge. She was ordained as a priest in 2004. She works on the narration of life stories, especially as they have influenced the writing (and reading) of exemplary and devotional lives since the late fifteenth century, in order to try to understand how this history has influenced our current understanding of what biography is and does. She is the author of *Walton's Lives: Conformist Commemorations and the Rise of Biography* (Oxford University Press, 2001). She is currently completing a Life of the Egyptologist, theologian and philosopher Margaret Benson (1865–1916).

The Revd Edmund Newey

Edmund Newey is Vicar of Saint Andrew's, Handsworth in Birmingham. Previously he worked as a schoolteacher in Bolton and as a parish priest in Manchester and Newmarket. He has published articles in journals such as *Modern Theology*, *Theology* and the *Anglican Theological Review*.

Revd Canon David Scott

David Scott is Rector of St Lawrence with St Swithun in Winchester, and Warden of the Diocesan School of Spirituality. He is also an Honorary Canon of Winchester Cathedral. Scott is an award-winning poet, having published a number of collections of poems including his latest, *Piecing Together* (Bloodaxe, 2005). He also has published collections of children's poems and has co-written a number of plays for the National Youth Music Theatre.

The Revd Canon Dr Andrew Shanks

Following 13 years in parish ministry, and a spell as a university lecturer, Andrew Shanks is now Canon Theologian at Manchester Cathedral. Among his various books on philosophical theology is a study of priesthood: *The Other Calling* (Blackwell, 2007).

The Revd Canon Dr Samuel Wells

Samuel Wells is Dean of the Chapel at Duke University and Research Professor of Christian Ethics at Duke Divinity School. He previously spent 14 years in parish ministry in the Church of England. He has written several books on theological ethics, including *God's Companions* (Blackwell, 2006).

The Revd Canon Dr Peter Wilcox

Peter Wilcox is Canon Chancellor at Lichfield Cathedral. He was previously a parish priest in Walsall and Gateshead. He is the author of *Living the Dream: Joseph for Today* (Paternoster, 2006).

The Most Revd Rowan Williams

Rowan Williams is the Archbishop of Canterbury. He was formerly Lady Margaret Professor of Divinity at Oxford University and the Archbishop of Wales. He is the author, among other books, of *Lost Icons*, *Teresa of Avila* and *Grace and Necessity*, all published by Continuum.

Index

Abolitionism 142–5
Adam 40
agapé 141
All Souls' Day services 100–4
Alternative Service Book 95
Anabaptists 136
'Angel of the North' 56
Anglicanism 5–10, 15, 136, 140,
    152–5, 159, 168, 189
antinomianism 141–2
antisemitism 127–30, 138, 141
Armistead, Margaret 189–90
assimilationism 165
'attention' 107–8
attention deficit hyperactivity
    disorder 74

baptism 160–4
Beckham, David 54
Bell, Catherine 4, 19
Bell, John 99
Bellos, Alex 56–7
bereavement 86–105
Berryman, Jerome 70–1, 84
Best, George 47, 58
blood-libel, the 128

Bonhoeffer, Dietrich 12
Brazilian national football team
    46
Bristol 143
British Broadcasting Corporation
    (BBC) 23
Busby, Matt 58

Calvinism 136
capital punishment *see* death
    penalty
Carr, Maxine 34
cathedral congregations 61
Cavalletti, Sofia 70–5, 84
Chapeltown 131
Chapman, Jessica 34
Charlton, Bobby 58
Cherry, Stephen 3, 23, 191;
    author of Chapter 1
children
    in church 71–7
    funerals of 97–9
Christian identity 81
Christian mission 133–5
Christian symbolism and imagery
    129–30, 133, 172

church attendance   155
church buildings   10–13, 24–5, 37,
      94, 105, 150, 177
Church of England   5, 15, 42, 51,
      72, 90, 126–7, 131–2, 147,
      151–61, 167–8, 178–9
   privileged status of   136
Clarkson, Thomas   144
Coakley, Edith   190
Coakley, Sarah   187–9, 191;
         author of Introduction and
         co-editor
Coldplay   93
Common Worship order   94–5,
      101
Communion, sharing of   140
community, sense of   83–4
confirmation   156, 160, 163–4
congregations   61, 66–71, 75–81,
      98–9
Conn, David   49
court proceedings   30–4
Craig, Gillean   177
Cromwell, Oliver   129
Cross of St George   172
crucifixion   129, 133, 144, 174

Darby, John Nelson   137
Davie, Grace   2, 4, 95, 191–2;
         author of Chapter 7
death penalty   31, 129
democratic processes   165
developing countries   151
Dickens, Charles   82, 84
Donne, John   103
Dowd, Mark   57–9
Dreamers, the   126

drug addiction   108–23

élites, religious and secular   158,
      166–7
Enlightenment thinking   150, 152
Equiano, Olaudah   144
establishment of the church   5,
      147–8, 166–9, 181
Ethiopia   130–2
Eucharist   28
Europe, contemporary religious
      situation in   153–61, 169
evangelicalism   167
excommunication   141

faith communities   166–9
Families Anonymous   118–19
Farrar, Austin   36
Fen Ditton   108–9
Ferguson, Alex   58
football   3, 41–64
   and belonging   55–8
   and the Church   61–4
   as idolatry   59–60, 63
   morality of   51–5
France   148–52, 157–8, 164–7
funerals and funeral ministry
      26–7, 34–9, 85, 89–101,
      104–5, 161–3

Glasgow Rangers and Glasgow
      Celtic   60
globalization   64
Gormley, Anthony   56
grace   4
group identities   165

Haile Selassie 130–2
Harries, Richard 18
Harrison, Robert 87–8, 104, 106
Hawnby 125–6
holiness 7–8, 104
Hollings, Michael 19
holy places 11–13
home, concept of 85–8, 93,
    104–5
homosexuality 4–5, 55, 140, 155,
    168
honesty, meaning of 138–41,
    144–5
hooliganism 60
hope as the priestly vocation 2
House of Lords 165–6
Huntley, Ian 34
hymns 93, 98

identity *see* Christian identity;
    group identities 187
imagination 83–4
immigration 157
incitement to religious hatred,
    legislation on 167
industrialization 149–52
Inge, John 11, 19

Jacobovits, Immanuel 128
Jesus Christ 87, 89, 130–4, 174–7,
    181–2
Jewish communities 127–30, 133,
    157
John, King 127
John Paul II, Pope 7
joy-riders 162–3
Judaism 130

kairos 100–1
Keane, Roy 62
kenosis 175
Kierkegaard, Søren 104
Kinnaird, Arthur 43

Lacoste, Jean-Yves 100, 106
Lambeth Conferences 7
Lang, Cosmo Gordon 7
Leicester University Department of
    Sociology 42, 55
Littlemore Conference 6, 10,
    14–19, 187–90
liturgy 76, 86–105, 134
  definition of 88
Liverpool 143
Liverpool FC 49
London bombings (July 2005) 158
Loughborough 21, 35
lumières 150
Lupson, Peter 43
Lutheranism 136, 164
Lynn, Vera 93

Malebiase, Hugh de 127
Malebiase, Richard de 127–8
Manchester 142–4
Manchester United 45–8, 58, 62
Maradona, Diego 53
Marion, Jean-Luc 10
Mark, St 134
Martin, Jessica 3, 192; *author of*
    Chapter 5
Martin, Michael 190
Milton, John 113–14
ministry *see* funerals and funeral
    ministry; pastoral ministry;

priesthood, the; prison
    ministry; representational
    ministry
Montessori tradition   70, 73
Moore, Alan   110
moral climate and moral codes
    154–5
Morrell, Adam   25–35, 38–9
Morris, Desmond   47, 50, 55–6, 60
multiculturalism   172
Muslim communities   157–8
Mussolini, Benito   131

Narcotics Anonymous   111, 119
Newcastle United   56–60
Newey, Edmund   3, 192; *author of
    Chapter 4*
Newman, John Henry   136, 189
Niebuhr, Reinhold   118
nonconformism   151
Norwich   82–3
Numeiry, Gaafar   130

ordained ministry   *see* priesthood

Paradise Lost   113–14
parish system   149, 152–4, 160–1,
    188
Parsons, Talcott   13–14
Pastoral Epistles   142
pastoral ministry   37, 147, 178, 181
Paul, St   40, 64, 101, 141–2
Pelé   53
Peter, St   93
place, significance of   10–11, 181
pluralism, religious   165–6
Poulat, Émile   158

poverty   13–15, 19, 82–3, 188
prayer   5–10, 92–4, 107–8
priesthood, the
    engagement in prayer   7–9
    'invisibility' of   4–5, 85
    of Jesus   175–6
    need for   173–5
    personal aspect of   107
    power of   65
    role of   1–4, 21–6, 32–9, 85–92,
        104–5, 131–2, 173, 176, 179–81
Priestley, J. B.   43
prison ministry   79–81
professionalism in the Church and
    elsewhere   62
propaganda, religious   132–40
public conscience movements
    144–5

Ramsey, Michael   100
Rastafarianism   131–2
referees in football   51–2
religion, nature of   43–5
religiosity   13
representational ministry   36–40,
    147
Richard III   127
ritual, power of   19
Robson, Sir Bobby   57
Rodwell, John   19
role models   59
Roman Catholicism   14, 70,
    136–7, 151, 168
Ronaldo, Christiano   45–6, 54
Rooney, Wayne   46, 54
Rose, Gillian   23
Royal Family, British   165–6

rugby players 51–2
Ryedale 125–7

Schünemann, Bernhard 16–18,
189–90
Scott, David 11, 90–2, 183–6, 190,
192–3
secularization 19, 147, 159, 163–6
separation of church and state
150
sermons 81
sexism 55
Shankly, Bill 44
Shanks, Andrew 2, 193; *author of
Chapter 6*
Sheba, Queen of 131
Sikhism 157
Silouan, Staretz 23
Sky TV 22
slavery and the slave trade 132,
142–5
sociology of religion 10
Soham murders 34
Solomon, King 131
Spain 151
sport 49; *see also* football
storytelling in church 67–70, 74–81
Struther, Ian 85–6
Swift, Graham 11

Taylor, Charles 19
Taylor Report 48, 50
television 63
Teresa, Mother 7
theology 136–40, 160, 188
Thomas, R. S. 9, 105
thoughtfulness 134–5

Tomlin, Graham 58

Underhill, Evelyn 7–9
United Nations 42
United States 5–6, 10, 13–14, 41,
151–2

vandalism 14
veils, wearing of 157
The Vicar of Dibley 2
'vicarious religion' 154–6, 166
Vico, Giambattista 88, 98
vocation, priestly 36, 188
Voltaire 150

Waban, Mass. 14, 187
Wallis, Ian 162–3
Watson, Christopher 190
Wedmeyer, Maria von 12
Wells, Holly 34
Wells, Samuel 3, 187–9, 193;
*author of Chapter 3 and note
on Littlemore Conference and
co-editor*
Welsh, Matthew 33
Wesley, John 125–6
Wilcox, Peter 3, 193; *author of
Chapter 2*
Williams, Robbie 98
Williams, Rowan 1, 85, 187–90,
193; *author of Epilogue*
Winner, David 54–7
women priests 2, 13
Wright, Bernard 31

Yom Tob 128
York 127–8